SRA
Reading Mastery
Signature Edition

Textbook A

Siegfried Engelmann
Susan Hanner

 SRA

A Division of The McGraw-Hill Companies
Columbus, OH

Illustration Credits
Dave Blanchette, Mark Corcoran, Susan DeMarco, John
Edwards and Associates, Kersti Frigell, Simon Galkin,
Meryl Henderson, Susan Jerde, Loretta Lustig, Steve
McComber, Pat Schories, Lauren Simeone, James Shough,
Rachel Taylor, and Gary Undercuffler.

SRAonline.com

 SRA

A Division of The McGraw-Hill Companies

Send all inquiries to this address:
SRA/McGraw-Hill
4400 Easton Commons
Columbus, OH 43219

ISBN: 978-0-07-612541-8
MHID: 0-07-612541-6

7 8 9 10 QPD 13 12 11 10 09

Table of Contents

A

1
1. rule
2. page
3. people
4. tiger
5. striped
6. straight

2
1. babies
2. flies
3. kittens
4. spiders

3
1. water
2. living
3. through
4. sugar

B Living Things

Here is a rule about all living things: **All living things grow, and all living things need water.**

Are trees living things? Yes. So you know that trees grow and trees need water.

Dogs are living things. So do dogs grow? Do dogs need water?

People are living things. Do people grow? Do people need water?

Here is another rule about all living things: **All living things make babies.**

Trees are living things. So trees make baby trees.
Are fish living things? So what do fish make?
Are spiders living things? So what do spiders make?
Remember the rule: All living things make babies.

C **Number your paper from 1 through 13.**

1. What do all living things need?

2. What do all living things make?

3. Do all living things grow?

4. Are flies living things?

5. Write the letters of **3** things you know about flies.
   a. Flies need water.   d. Flies need ants.
   b. Flies need sugar.   e. Flies make babies.
   c. Flies grow.

6. Are dogs living things?

7. So you know that dogs need ▮▮▮▮.

8. And you know that dogs make ▮▮▮▮.

9. Are chairs living things?

10. Do chairs need water?

D The Tiger and the Frog

Tom's brother had two pets. One pet was a frog. The other pet was a big mean tiger. Tom's brother kept his pets in boxes. One day Tom said, "I want to play with your pet frog."

Tom's brother said, "Here is the rule about where I keep that frog. **I keep the frog in the box that is striped.**" Then Tom's brother said, "Don't get mixed up, because I keep my pet tiger in one of the other boxes."

Tom said the rule to himself. Then he went into the room with the boxes.

Here is what Tom saw.

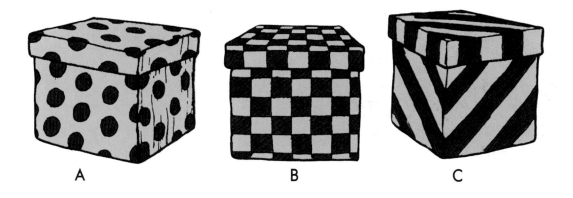

A   B   C

Tom looked at box A. He tried to think of the rule his brother had told him.

Is box A striped?

So is the frog inside box A?

Tom looked at box B.

Is box B striped?

So is the frog inside box B?

Tom looked at box C. After looking at all the boxes, Tom opened box B.

Did a frog hop out of box B?

Turn to the next page and you will see what happened.

E **Story Items**

11. What's the title of today's story?
    - The Tiger and the Dog
    - The Tiger and the Frog
    - The Dog and the Frog

12. Name **2** pets that Tom's brother had.

13. Did Tom open the right box?

A

1	2	3
1. whole	1. through	1. striped
2. moop	2. straight	2. pointed
3. carry	3. forest	3. wise
4. covered	4. field	4. strange
5. make-believe	5. page	
6. facts		

B # Make-Believe Animals

Here's a real animal.   Here's a make-believe animal.

What parts of the animal are make-believe?

The story you'll read today tells about animals called moops. Moops are make-believe animals. That means there are not really any moops.

C Number your paper from 1 through 9.

1. Write the letter of each make-believe animal.

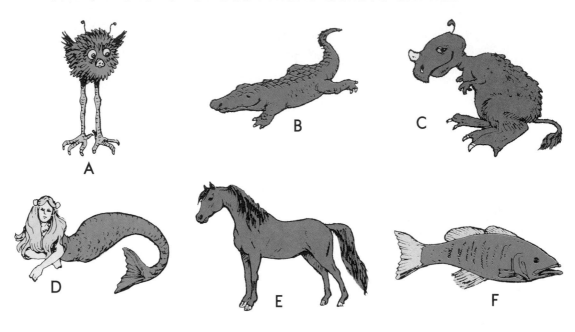

A

B

C

D

E

F

D Bob and Don Find Moops

Don and Bob lived near a strange forest. There were many strange animals in the forest. One strange animal was a moop. Moops were little animals with long hair. They made very good pets.

One day Don and Bob went out to get pet moops. On the path through the forest they met a wise old man. The wise old man said, "A moop makes a good pet. But do not cut a moop's hair. Here's the rule about a moop: **The more you cut its hair, the faster its hair grows.**"

Don listened to the old man. But Bob did not listen.

Don found a pet moop, and Bob found a pet moop. Don took his pet moop home and put it in a box. Bob took his pet moop home and looked at it. Bob said, "The hair on this moop is too long. So I will cut it." Bob started to cut the moop's hair, but the hair started to grow back. So Bob cut more hair. But the more he cut the hair, the faster the hair grew.

Soon the moop's hair was so long that it filled the room. Soon the hair was so long that Bob could not find his moop.

Don kept his moop for years. Don had a lot of fun with his moop. But Bob did not have fun with his moop. He never found his moop. All he could see was a room full of hair.

THE END

E Story Items

2. What is the title of today's story?
   - Moops Find Bob and Don
   - Bob and Don Find Moops
   - Bob and Don Find Mops

3. Write the 2 missing words.

   The wise old man said, "The more you cut its ▨▨▨, the ▨▨▨ its hair grows."

4. Who did not listen to the wise old man?

5. What happened to the moop's hair when Bob cut it?

6. Did Bob have fun with his moop?

7. Are moops **real** or **make-believe?**

8. One of the pictures shows Don's moop in a room. Write the letter of that picture.

9. One of the pictures shows Bob's moop in a room. Write the letter of that picture.

A   B   C   D

3

A

1
1. great
2. danger
3. destroy
4. grove
5. measure
6. weight

2
1. <u>make</u>-believe
2. <u>together</u>
3. <u>during</u>
4. <u>howled</u>
5. <u>branches</u>

3
1. covered
2. washed
3. pointed
4. crashed
5. cracked

4
1. twig
2. during
3. carry
4. ground
5. facts
6. bark

5
1. roots
2. trunk
3. whole
4. ripe
5. flowers

B Trees

Trees have roots. The roots are under the ground. The roots do two things. The roots hold the tree up to keep it from falling over. The roots also carry water from the ground to all parts of the tree. Trees could not live if they did not have roots.

roots

PICTURE 1

Here's another fact about trees. Trees do not grow in the winter because the ground is cold. In the spring, trees start to grow. The sun makes the ground warmer in the spring. First the top of the ground gets warm. Then the deeper parts of the ground get warm.

Small trees begin to grow before big trees grow. Small trees grow first because their roots are not very deep in the ground. Their roots are in warmer ground. So their roots warm up before the roots of big trees warm up.

PICTURE 2

C Number your paper from 1 through 17.
1. What part of a tree is under the ground?
2. Roots keep the tree from ▭.
3. Roots carry ▭ to all parts of the tree.
4. Could trees live if they didn't have roots?
5. When do trees begin to grow?
   • in the winter   • in the spring

6. Trees begin to grow when their roots get .

Look at
these trees.

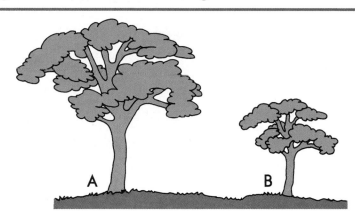

A   B

7. Write the letter of the tree that has deeper roots.

8. Write the letter of the tree that begins to grow first every year.

9. Which letter in the picture below shows where the ground gets warm first?

10. Which letter shows where the ground gets warm last?

Ⓓ Don Washes the White Spot

Don had a pretty white coat. But he didn't like white coats. He wanted a blue coat. Don said, "I'll buy a blue coat." So he started to walk to town. He had to walk through the strange forest to get to town. Don met the wise old man on the path through the forest. Don told the wise old man, "I'm on my way to get a blue coat."

The wise old man said, "I will give you a blue coat." The wise old man held up a pretty blue coat.

The coat had one little white spot on it. The old man pointed to the spot and said, "Do not try to wash this spot away. Here's the rule: **The more you wash this spot, the bigger it will get.**"

Don did not listen to the old man. Don took the pretty blue coat home. Then he said to himself, "I don't like that little spot on the coat. I will wash it away."

So Don got some soap and water. Then he started to wash the spot. He washed a little bit and the spot got a little bigger. Don washed some more. And the white spot got bigger. Don washed and washed and washed. And the spot got bigger and bigger and bigger. The more Don washed, the bigger the spot got.

Soon the white spot was so big that it covered the whole coat. The whole coat was white. Now Don did not have a white coat and a blue coat. He had two white coats. Don said, "I hate white coats."

THE END

E Story Items

11. What's the title of today's story?
   - Don Washes the Moop
   - Don Washes the White Spot
   - Don Spots the White Moop

12. Did Don like white coats?

13. The old man said, "The more you wash this spot, the ▬▬▬ it will get."

14. What color was the coat that the old man gave Don?

15. What happened to the spot when Don washed it?

16. What color was the coat after Don washed it?

17. Write the letter of the picture that shows a forest.

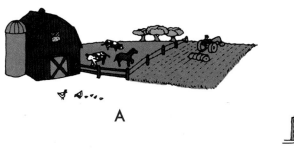

A

B

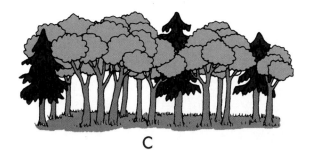

C

D

A

1
1. alive
2. seasons
3. terrible
4. millions
5. measure
6. weight

2
1. during
2. blowing
3. cheering
4. glowing
5. growing

3
1. <u>apple</u>
2. <u>loved</u>
3. <u>greatest</u>
4. <u>meaner</u>
5. <u>cracked</u>
6. <u>crashed</u>

4
1. grove
2. bark
3. trunk
4. howled
5. branches
6. care

5
1. pretty
2. twig
3. ripe
4. flowers
5. Tina
6. destroy

B Apple Trees

Apple trees are different from forest trees. Forest trees are tall and straight. Apple trees are short and not so straight. Forest trees have very small branches. Apple trees have large branches.

Here is a forest tree.

Here is an apple tree.

Apple trees have white flowers in the spring. Later, in the summer, a little apple starts growing from each place where there was a flower.

By the fall, the apples are big and ripe. They will fall off if they are not picked. The leaves also fall off in the fall. During the winter, the apple tree does not grow. It is in a kind of sleep. It will start growing again in the spring.

The pictures below show a twig of an apple tree in the spring, the summer, the fall, and the winter.

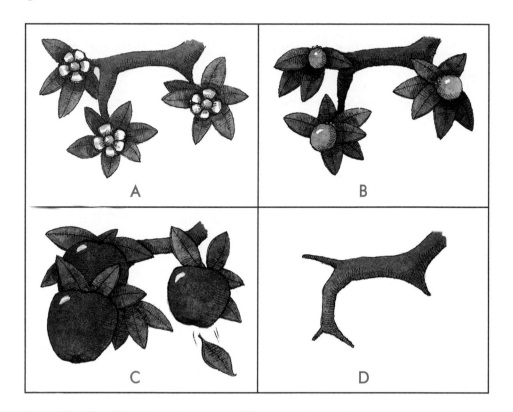

C **Number your paper from 1 through 17.**

1. What color are the flowers that apple trees make?

   • red   • white   • blue

2. When do those flowers come out?

   • fall   • summer   • spring

3. What grows in each place where there was a flower?

4. Which has a tall straight trunk, a forest tree or an apple tree?

   • forest tree   • apple tree

5. Which has larger branches, a forest tree or an apple tree?

   • forest tree   • apple tree

D   The Little Apple Tree

Tina was an apple tree. She loved to hold her leaves out to the sun. She loved to make green leaves and pretty white flowers in the spring. She loved to make big red apples in the fall. And she loved to have a great big sleep every winter.

But Tina didn't get to do all the things she loved to do. She didn't live in a nice grove of apple trees. She lived in a forest with big mean trees that didn't care about her. Those big trees took all of the sunshine they could reach. And they didn't leave much for Tina. They dropped leaves and bark and seeds and branches all over little Tina.

When the wind started blowing, the big trees would swing and howl and have lots of fun. They didn't let the wind reach Tina.

And those big trees didn't care what Tina said.

One spring day, she said, "Please stop dropping things on me. I am trying to make white flowers."

One of the big trees said, "She doesn't want us to do **this.**" That tree dropped a small branch right on Tina.

Another big tree said, "Ho, ho. She doesn't want us to do **this.**" That tree dropped a bigger branch on Tina.

The biggest tree said, "Ho, ho. She really doesn't want us to do **this**." That tree dropped the biggest branch it had. That branch crashed down on top of Tina. It cracked two of Tina's branches.

The big trees howled and said, "That was good. We really dropped some big ones on that apple tree. Ho, ho."

MORE NEXT TIME

E Story Items

6. What's the title of today's story?
   - The Mean Trees
   - The Little Apple Tree
   - How Apples Grow

7. How many apple trees were near Tina?
   - 26   • none   • one

8. Who kept the wind and the sunlight away from Tina?
   - the wind   • the rain   • the tall trees

For items 9 through 12, read each thing that Tina did. Then write the season that tells when she did it.
   - winter   • spring   • summer   • fall

9. Made big red apples
10. Made leaves and white flowers
11. Made little apples where each flower was
12. Went to sleep

13. Write 3 things the big trees dropped on Tina.
- bark
- apples
- bottles
- boxes
- branches
- leaves
- cans

The pictures show the same twig in 4 seasons. **Write the name of the season for each twig.**

14.

15.

16.

17.

5

1
1. hoof
2. hooves
3. true
4. sure
5. fence
6. agree

2
1. <u>seasons</u>
2. <u>camp</u>er
3. <u>matt</u>er
4. <u>glow</u>ing
5. <u>grow</u>ing

3
1. millions
2. greatest
3. blowing
4. knocked
5. meaner

4
1. terrible
2. cheering
3. curly
4. campfire
5. alive

5
1. animals
2. destroy
3. another
4. danger

B Forest Fires

A forest is a place with lots of tall trees that are close together. The inside of a forest is very dark.

Sometimes, a forest burns. That's called a forest fire. Here are facts about forest fires.

The danger of a forest fire is greatest in the fall.

The danger of a forest fire is not very great in the winter or spring. In these seasons things are wet and trees do not have dry leaves.

The danger of a forest fire is not very great in the summer because the leaves on the trees are alive. So they are not dry.

In the fall, the leaves die and become dry. Many dry leaves are on the ground in the fall. So if a small fire starts, it may grow larger as it moves through the dry leaves on the ground. Soon, that fire may leap up into the trees and become a terrible forest fire.

Forest fires kill wild animals and trees. Large forest fires may burn for weeks. They may destroy millions of trees. And it may take more than 200 years for the forest to grow back.

C Number your paper from 1 through 15.

1. In which season is the danger of forest fires greatest?
   - winter
   - spring
   - summer
   - fall

2. In the fall, are the leaves on trees dead or alive?
   - dead
   - alive

3. Are dead leaves wet or dry?
   - wet
   - dry

4. In summer, are the leaves on trees dead or alive?
   - dead
   - alive

5. Are those leaves wet or dry?
   - wet
   - dry

6. A forest fire may burn for ▮▮▮▮.
   - minutes
   - weeks
   - hours

7. A forest fire kills both ▮▮▮▮ and ▮▮▮▮.
   - plants
   - animals
   - fish
   - whales

8. About how many years could it take for the forest to grow back?
   - 100 years
   - 20 years
   - 200 years

D Campers Come into the Forest

Tina was very sad all summer and all fall. The only thing the big trees let Tina do was sleep when winter came. They went to sleep too. But in the spring when Tina woke up and tried to make little green leaves, the big trees started dropping things and making jokes.

"That apple tree doesn't like it when we do **this,**" they would say and then drop something on her.

Things were bad all spring and all summer.

On one fall day, the trees were meaner than ever. Tina had made lots of big red apples. The big trees were trying to drop branches on her and knock off her apples.

They would say, "She doesn't like it when we do **this,**" and they would drop a branch. If the branch knocked off an apple, the big trees would cheer. This game went on until the big trees had no more branches they could let go of. Poor Tina had only three apples left.

Just then three campers came into the forest. They made a fire. The big trees got scared.

One big tree said, "What is the matter with those campers? Don't they know they should not make fires in the fall?"

Another big tree said, "Yes, things are dry. And we hate forest fires."

After a while, the campers put dirt on the fire and started to leave. They didn't see that part of the fire was still glowing.

"Oh, no," one of the trees said, as the campers were leaving. "That fire will start up as soon as the wind blows."

Another tree said, "And it will make a forest fire. And we will burn up."

MORE NEXT TIME

E Story Items

9. Did Tina feel happy or sad? • happy • sad
10. What did the big trees do to knock off her apples?
    - dropped boxes on her
    - yelled at her
    - dropped branches
11. How many apples did she have left at the end of the game?
    - 26 • 3 • 1
12. The big trees didn't knock off the rest of her apples because they didn't have any more ▓▓▓.
    - time • money • things to drop
13. Who came to the forest at the end of the game?
    - an apple tree • a bear • campers
14. What did the campers make?
    - a fire • a house • a hut
15. The big trees saw something the campers did not see. What was that?
    - Tina • a glowing fire • a hot rock

A

1
1. thousand
2. should
3. touch
4. half
5. centimeter
6. remove

2
1. <u>camp</u>fire
2. <u>some</u>thing
3. <u>any</u>thing
4. <u>sun</u>shine
5. <u>with</u>out

3
1. garden
2. shout
3. proud
4. shame
5. flames
6. waded

4
1. agree
2. true
3. camel
4. bonk
5. hoof
6. stream

5
1. hump
2. hooves
3. curly
4. fence
5. sure
6. tadpole

B

Camels and Pigs

In the next lesson, you'll read about a camel and a pig. Camels and pigs are the same in some ways and different in some ways. Both camels and pigs have hooves.

Here's a pig's hoof.

Here's a camel's hoof.

The pig's nose and the camel's nose are different.

Which animal has this nose?

Which animal has this nose?

The back of each animal is different. One of the animals has a large hump on its back.

A camel's tail and a pig's tail are different. One animal has a long tail. The other animal has a short curly tail.

One of the animals is very big and the other animal is much, much smaller. Here they are, side by side.

C Tina Is Happy

The trees were afraid of a forest fire. A campfire was glowing, and it would make flames as soon as the wind started blowing. The campers who made the fire were leaving. As they walked away, the big trees shouted at each other, "Drop something on those campers. Make them stop and go back."

But the trees didn't have anything to drop. They had dropped all their old branches and leaves on Tina. The campers were now walking under Tina's branches.

The big trees called, "Tina, save us. Save us. Drop something on those campers."

"Yes," a  big tree said, "if you save us we'll be good to you for 100 years."

Tina hated to drop her only three apples, but she did. They landed on the campers: bonk, bonk, bonk. The campers stopped and bent over to pick up the apples.

One of the campers looked back at the fire and said, "We didn't put out that fire. Shame on us."

They went back and made sure that the fire was out before they left.

So now, Tina is happy. The big trees don't drop things on her. In the spring those trees bend far to the side so the sun can reach Tina.

Hey, stop taking Tina's sunshine.

Tina can make green leaves and pretty white flowers. If one of the big trees holds a branch out and keeps the sun from reaching her, the other big trees say, "Hey, move your branch. You're taking Tina's sunshine."

And in the fall, those trees are very proud when Tina makes apples—lots and lots of big red apples. "Look at all those apples," they say. "And we helped her make them. Good for us."

Those big trees agree about how much Tina did for them. They say, "Tina gave up her only three apples to save us, so we love that little apple tree."

THE END

D Number your paper from 1 through 17.

Some of these parts belong to a **cow.** Some of them belong to a **camel.** And some belong to a **pig. Write the name of the animal that has the part shown in each picture.**

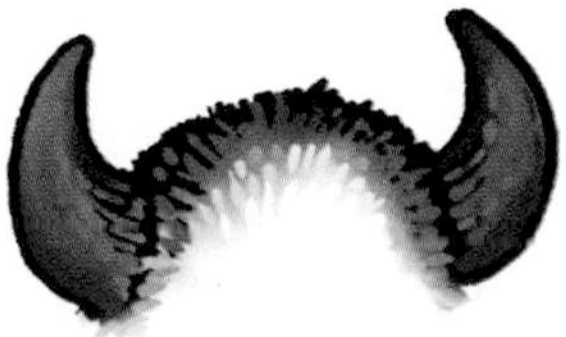

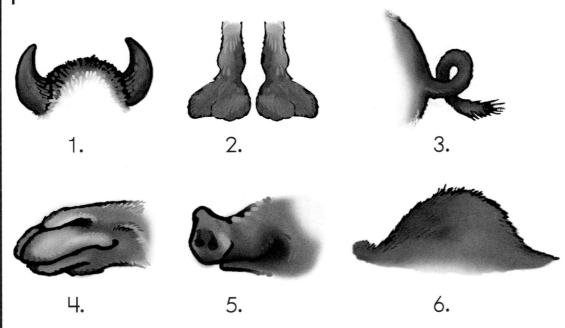

1.

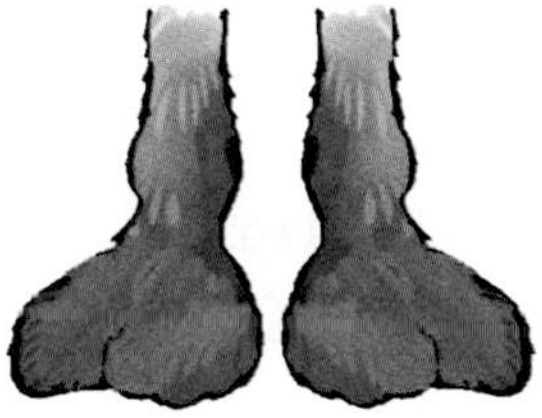

2.

3.

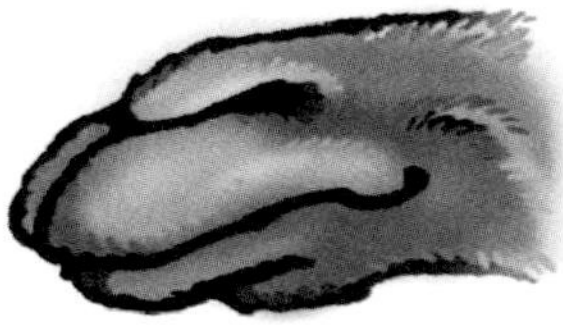

4.

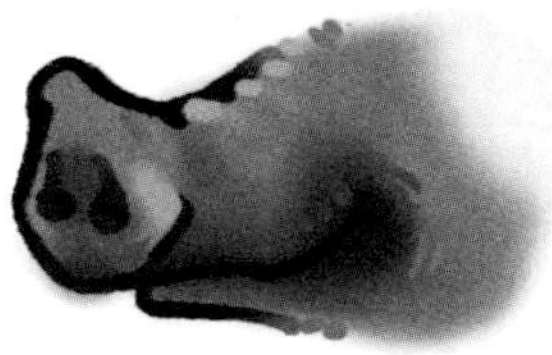

5.

6.

7. Which is bigger, a camel or a pig?
8. Which has a longer tail, a camel or a pig?

E Story Items

9. The big trees didn't drop something on the campers because they didn't have any more ______.
    - time
    - money
    - things to drop

10. The big trees wanted someone to help them. Who was that?

   • a big tree   • a farmer   • Tina

11. The big trees told Tina that they would be good to her for ▐▐▐ years.

   • 30   • 100   • 500

12. How many apples did Tina have before she dropped some?

13. How many apples did she drop?

14. What did one camper see when he was picking up an apple?

   • the campfire   • Tina   • the tall trees

15. Did the campers put out the fire?

16. Do the big trees still do mean things to Tina?

17. Write the letters for the 2 things the big trees do to make sure that Tina gets lots of sunshine.

   a. move their branches so Tina gets sunlight
   b. make shadows
   c. drop bark and branches
   d. bend to the side

A

1
1. ce
2. ou
3. ir

2
1. ground
2. pound
3. around
4. race
5. place
6. fence

3
1. <u>in</u>side
2. <u>without</u>
3. <u>ugl</u>iest
4. <u>touching</u>

4
1. sure
2. easy
3. should
4. right
5. half

5
1. thousand
2. promise
3. centimeter
4. garden
5. people

B **More Facts About** Camels

In today's lesson, you'll read about camels and pigs. Here are some facts about camels.

Most camels live in places that are very dry. Sometimes there is no rain for years in these places.

The camels work like trucks that carry things.

Camels do a good job because they can go for ten days without drinking water. That's because they can drink a lot of water at one time and store that water in their body. A camel that is 1 thousand pounds can drink as much as 250 pounds of water at one time.

The hooves of camels are very wide and flat, so these hooves don't sink in the sand.

Some people ride camels the way we ride horses, and people even have camel races.

C The Camel and the Pig

Is it better to be tall or better to be short? A pig and a camel did not agree. The camel said, "It is easy to see that it is better to be tall."

"No, that is not true," the pig said. "It is far better to be short than to be tall."

Soon, the camel and the pig were yelling at each other. "It's better to be tall," the camel shouted.

"No way," the pig shouted. "Short is better, better, better."

At last a cow became tired of all this shouting and yelling. She said to the camel, "If tall is better, you should be able to show us why it is better." Then she said to the pig, "If short is better, you should be able to show us why it is better." ✦ Then the cow said, "If you do not win, you must give something to the one who wins."

The camel said, "I am so sure that I am right, I will give the pig my hump if I do not win."

The pig said, "And I am so sure I am right, I will give up my nose and my tail."

So the camel and the pig went out to see who was right. They came to a garden with a fence around it. Inside were good things to eat.

The camel said, "I am tall. So it is easy for me to reach over the top and eat all I want." And she ate and ate and ate.

The pig did not eat because she could not reach over the fence.

MORE NEXT TIME

D Number your paper from 1 through 12.

1. Camel hooves keep camels from sinking in sand. How are camel hooves different from pig hooves?
   - They are sharper and smaller.
   - They are wider and flatter.
   - They are harder and longer.

2. Are camels used more in **wet places** or **dry places?**
   - wet places
   - dry places

3. Camels can go for ▮▮▮ days without drinking water.

4. How many pounds of water can a 1 thousand-pound camel drink at one time? ▮▮▮ pounds.

E Story Items

5. What's the title of this story?
   - The Cow and the Horse
   - How Animals are Different
   - The Camel and the Pig

6. Which animal believed that tall was better?
   - pig
   - cow
   - camel

7. Which animal believed that short was better?

     • pig   • cow   • camel

8. Which animal got tired of the yelling and shouting?

     • pig   • cow   • camel

9. What did the camel agree to give up if she was not right?

     • hooves   • hump   • head

10. What did the pig agree to give up if she was not right?

     • teeth   • nose   • tail

11. Which animal was able to eat at the garden?

     • camel   • pig   • cow

12. Why was she able to eat from the garden?
- She could open the gate.
- She could jump over the fence.
- She could reach over the fence.

1
1. writing
2. William
3. apartment
4. construction

2
1. ugliest
2. pencils
3. touching
4. without
5. centimeters
6. tadpoles

3
1. cent
2. chances
3. faces
4. races
5. dances

4
1. half
2. eaten
3. both
4. peeking
5. promise
6. remove

5
1. erase
2. eraser
3. ink
4. shaft
5. tipped
6. cloth

B Facts About Centimeters

The story you're going to read tells about centimeters. Here are facts about centimeters:

- Centimeters are used to tell how long things are.
- Inches also tell how long things are. An inch is longer than a centimeter.

  Here's an inch: _____

  Here's a centimeter: ___

Hold up your fingers and show your teacher how long an inch is.

Now show your teacher how long a centimeter is.

C The Camel and the Pig Trade Parts

The camel had just eaten from a garden. The cow said, "The camel showed that tall is better."

"No," the pig said. "There is another garden down the road. We must go there and I will show you that short is better."

So the camel and the pig and the cow went to the next garden. It had a very high wall, with a hole near the ground. The pig went in the hole and ate good things that were in the garden. The camel didn't eat because the wall was too high.

When the pig came back from the garden, the cow said, "Well, the pig showed that short is better."

"I win," the pig said.

"No, I win," the camel said.

The cow said to the camel, "The pig showed you that short is better. You agreed to give up your hump. So give it up."

Then the cow said to the pig, "The camel showed you that tall is better. You agreed to give up your nose and your tail. So give them to the camel."

The camel and the pig were very sad, but they did what they promised they would do. ★ The pig got a great big hump. The camel got a pig's nose and a pig's tail.

The pig looked at the camel and said, "You look bad. That nose and tail don't fit you at all. And you look silly without a hump."

The camel said to the pig, "You don't even have a nose or a tail, and you've got a hump that is bigger than the rest of you."

The cow said, "I will let both of you take back the things you gave up, but you must promise not to yell and fight anymore."

The camel and the pig agreed.

So the camel took back her hump and the pig took back her nose and tail. Then the cow said, "You both look a lot better. And I'm glad that we will not have to hear any more talk about tall and short."

The pig said, "I agree that it is better to be tall some times, but most of the time short is way better than tall."

The camel said, "Not true. Most of the time it's better to be tall than short."

"Oh, no," the cow said and walked away.

THE END

D Number your paper from 1 through 12.

1. Which is longer, an inch or a centimeter?

- an inch   - a centimeter

2. Some of the lines in the box are one inch long. Some of the lines are one centimeter long. **Write the letter of every line that is one inch long.**

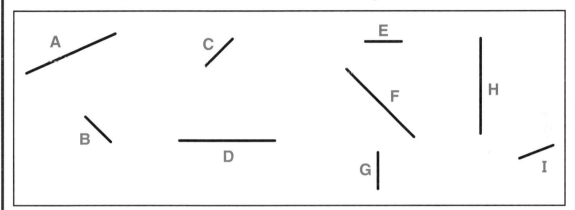

3. Write the letter of every line that is one centimeter long.

E Story Items

4. What did the camel agree to give up if she was not right?

- hump   - hooves   - head

5. What did the pig agree to give up if she was not right?

- teeth   - tail   - nose

6. Who ate at the first garden?

- camel   • cow   • pig

7. Who ate at the next garden?

- camel   • cow   • pig

8. How did the pig get food from this garden?

- jumped over the wall
- went through a hole
- opened the gate

9. Which parts did the pig give to the camel?

- hump   • nose
- feet   • tail

10. Which part did the camel give to the pig?

- hump   • nose
- feet   • tail

11. Which animals promised not to argue about tall and short?

- goat   • cow   • toad   • pig
- horse   • fish   • dog   • camel

12. Did they keep their promise?

A

1
1. ruler
2. thought
3. escape
4. writing
5. tipped
6. stream

2
1. dance
2. prance
3. pencil
4. fence

3
1. Mary Williams
2. construction
3. apartment
4. eraser
5. escaping
6. waded

4
1. ink
2. erase
3. cloth
4. shaft
5. boast
6. boasted

B Felt-Tipped Pens

You'll read a story about a felt-tipped pen. Here are facts about felt-tipped pens:

- Felt-tipped pens have tips that are made of felt. Felt is a kind of cloth.
- The shaft of the pen is filled with ink. The shaft is the long part of the pen that you hold when you write.
- The ink flows down to the tip. Ink is wet. The tip is made of cloth. So when ink gets on the tip, the tip gets wet with ink.
- Most felt-tipped pens do not have an eraser. Ink is not easy to erase. What kind of writing tool does have an eraser?

C Joe Williams Wants a New Job

Joe Williams was a felt-tipped pen. He had a wide tip and his color was bright red. Joe's job was construction. He worked with other members of the construction team—pencils, paints, other pens, brushes, and erasers. Their construction job was to make pictures.

All day long, Joe worked with the others. They worked very fast. First, Joe would be sitting next to the other pens. Then somebody would pick him up, make a few marks with him, and toss him back with the other pens.

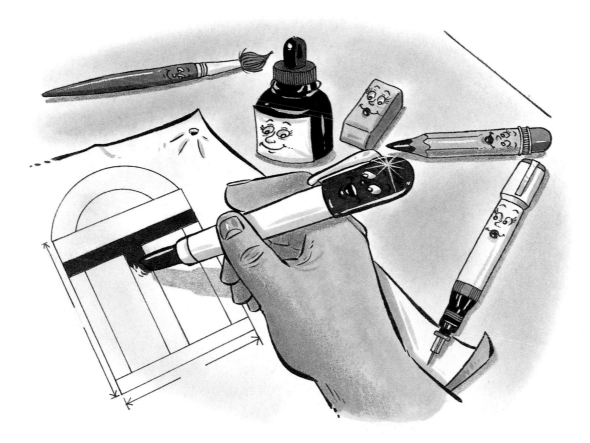

The work was hard, and everybody on the construction team was glad when it was time for lunch. The members of the team would sit and talk about the picture they were making. Then, at one o'clock, work would start again, and it would keep going until the end of the day.

After the work was done, Joe would go to his apartment. ✸ He lived in the desk with his wife, Mary, who worked as a number-one pencil.

Every day, the same thing happened. Joe worked on construction, laying down red lines and red marks. Then he went home. One day, Joe said to himself, "I'm tired of being a felt-tipped pen. I'm tired of laying down red lines. I want a new job."

❀ When Joe told his wife that he was thinking of taking up a new job, she said, "Don't be silly, Joe. What else can you do?" Joe looked at himself. He couldn't work as an eraser because he didn't have an eraser. He couldn't work as a pencil holder, because he didn't have the right shape. He couldn't work as a sheet of paper.

He said to himself, "Let's face it, Joe. You're just made to be a red felt-tipped pen." Then he said, "But I must be able to do something else."

Joe felt sad, but he didn't stop ❀ thinking about a new job.

MORE NEXT TIME

D Number your paper from 1 through 15.

1. Felt is a kind of ▬▬▬.
2. Most felt-tipped pens do not have an eraser because ink is ▬▬▬.

- wet
- hard to erase
- red

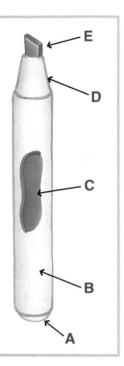

3. Which letter shows the ink?
4. Which letter shows the shaft?
5. Which letter shows the felt tip?
6. The pen in the picture does not have an eraser. Write the letter that shows where an eraser would go on the pen.

E Story Items

7. What color ink did Joe Williams have?
8. What kind of tip did Joe Williams have?
9. What kind of job did Joe have?

- making red lines
- making erasers
- making blue lines

10. Write the names of 3 other members of the construction team.
- cans
- pencils
- drills
- erasers
- brushes
- baskets

11. Where did Joe live?

12. His wife was named ████.

13. Did she think that Joe could get a new job?

14. One of the things in the picture could be Joe's wife. Write the letter of the object that could be Joe's wife.

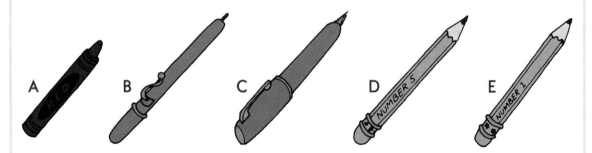

A B C D E

15. Object D could not be Joe's wife because Joe's wife is ████.

Number your paper from 1 through 24.

1. Are flies living things?

2. **Write the letters of 3** things you know about flies.

    a. Flies need ants.   d. Flies grow.

    b. Flies need sugar.   e. Flies make babies.

    c. Flies need water.

3. Roots keep a tree from ⬛⬛⬛.

4. Roots carry ⬛⬛⬛ to all parts of the tree.

5. When do trees begin to grow?

        • in the spring   • in the winter

6. Trees begin to grow when their roots get ⬛⬛⬛.

7. What color are the flowers that apple trees make?

8. When do those flowers come out?

9. What grows in each place where there was a flower?

10. In summer, are the leaves on trees dead or alive?

11. Are those leaves wet or dry?

12. Which is bigger, a camel or a pig?
13. Which has a longer tail, a camel or a pig?
14. Camels can go for ______ days without drinking water.
15. How many pounds of water can a 1 thousand-pound camel drink at one time?
16. Which is longer, a centimeter or an inch?
17. Some of the lines in the box are one inch long. Some of the lines are one centimeter long. **Write the letter** of every line that is one inch long.

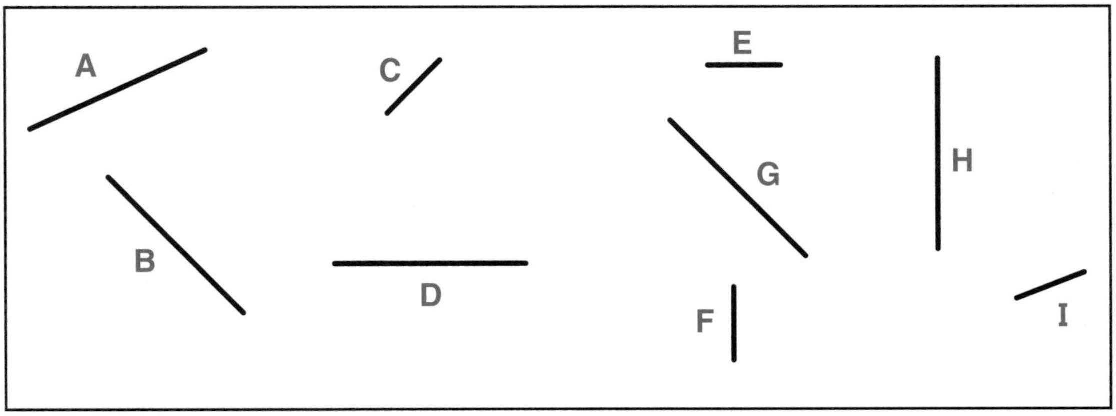

Skill Items

For each item, write the underlined word or words from the sentences in the box.

> You <u>measure</u> your <u>weight</u> in <u>pounds</u>.
> They <u>waded</u> into the stream to <u>remove</u> <u>tadpoles</u>.

18. What word names baby frogs or toads?
19. What word names the unit you use to measure weight?
20. What word tells how many pounds something is?
21. What word tells about taking things from the stream?
22. What word tells about walking in water that is not very deep?
23. What word tells what you do to find out how heavy or long something is?

24. **The more sunlight apple trees get, the more apples they make.** Write the letter of each tree that got lots of sunlight.

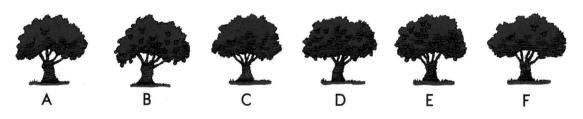

A   B   C   D   E   F

END OF TEST 1

1
1. circus
2. famous
3. human
4. blood
5. expensive
6. thousand

2
1. Martha Jumpjump
2. Henry Ouch
3. Aunt Fanny
4. Carl Goodscratch

3
1. bread
2. world
3. flea
4. fame
5. insect
6. boasted

4
1. round
2. ruler
3. dancing
4. hogged
5. thoughts
6. escaping

Centimeters

The story you'll read today tells about centimeters. Remember, **a centimeter is shorter than an inch.**

Every line in this row is one centimeter long:

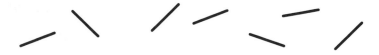

Every line in this row is one inch long:

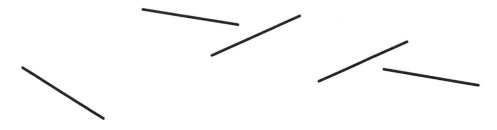

C Joe Williams Gets a New Job

Every night, Joe went home and thought about jobs that he might do, but he didn't come up with any good thoughts. Then one night, Joe had a good thought. He was watching his wife, Mary. She was singing to herself, and she was dancing. When a number-one pencil dances, she makes a little line on the floor. Then she jumps and makes another little line right next to the first line. As Joe watched her make these lines, he jumped up from the chair and jumped across the floor. "I've got it," he yelled. "I've got it!"

Mary stopped dancing and looked at Joe. "What are you thinking?"

Joe said, "I want you to make marks on me. Make marks that are one centimeter apart. Make marks all down the side of my shaft. If I have those marks on my shaft, I can work as a ruler."

Mary said, "Maybe that will work. Let's see."

She made the marks on Joe's side. Then she made numbers by the marks. When she was done, Joe jumped up and looked at himself. "Wow, that's nice," he said. He kept turning around and looking at himself. "I'll be the only round ruler on the construction team."

The next day, Joe didn't line up with the other pens. He went over with the rulers.

One ruler said, "What do you think you're doing here, pen?"

"I'm now a ruler," Joe said.

Another ruler said, "We'll soon find out if you're really a ruler. It's just about time to work."

Pretty soon, somebody picked up Joe and said, "Let's see how this round ruler works." The person used Joe as a ruler. "This round ruler works very well," the person said. And from that day on, Joe had a new job. He was a round ruler. And he was happy.

THE END

D Number your paper from 1 through 16.
Story Items

1. One of the things in the picture could be Joe's wife. Write the letter of the object that could be Joe's wife.

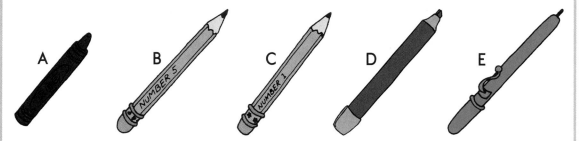

2. Object B could not be Joe's wife because Joe's wife is ▮▮▮▮.

Here's the rule: **The faster Mary dances, the shorter her lines.**

3. Write the letter of the lines Mary made when she danced the fastest.

4. Write the letter of the lines Mary made when she danced the slowest.

A   B   C   D   E

Skill Items

Use the words in the box to write complete sentences.

remove	weight	sing	waded
measure	tadpoles	pounds	circus

5. They ____ into the stream to ____ ____.
6. You ____ your ____ in ____.

Review Items

7. Which has a tall straight trunk, an apple tree or a forest tree?
   - apple tree
   - forest tree
8. Which has smaller branches, an apple tree or a forest tree?
   - apple tree
   - forest tree
9. A forest fire may burn for ____.
   - hours
   - minutes
   - weeks
10. A forest fire kills both ____ and ____.
   - plants
   - whales
   - fish
   - animals
11. About how many years could it take for the forest to grow back?
   - 20 years
   - 200 years
   - 100 years

12. Camel hooves keep camels from sinking in sand. How are camel hooves different from pig hooves?
- They are harder and longer.
- They are sharper and smaller.
- They are wider and flatter.

For items 13 through 16, read each thing that Tina did. Then write the season that tells when she did it.
- summer   • fall   • spring   • winter

13. Made leaves and white flowers

14. Went to sleep

15. Made big red apples

16. Made little apples where each flower was

1
1. Russia
2. great
3. surprise
4. tomorrow

2
1. Aunt Fanny
2. Carl Goodscratch
3. Henry Ouch
4. Martha Jumpjump

3
1. second
2. minute
3. hour
4. week

4
1. juggle
2. ladies
3. circus
4. famous

5
1. blood
2. bread
3. human
4. flea
5. world

6
1. thousands
2. gentlemen
3. expensive
4. insect
5. hogged

Facts About Fleas

You'll read about fleas in today's story. Here are some facts about fleas:

- Fleas are insects.
  All insects have six legs.
  So fleas have six legs.
- Fleas bite and suck blood.

- A row of about five big fleas is one centimeter long.
- Different kinds of fleas live on different kinds of animals.

Cat fleas like to live on cats. Cat fleas are different from dog fleas. Dog fleas are different from human fleas. Human fleas are different from rat fleas.

The picture below shows a dog flea.

real size

C Aunt Fanny's Flea Circus

Aunt Fanny's Flea Circus was formed in 1993. The circus had a great line-up of acts. Aunt Fanny had the most famous fleas in the world. One act was Carl Goodscratch, who dove 48 centimeters into two drops of water. When Carl did his dive, the people watching the show would sit without making a sound. Then they would cheer and stamp their feet. Another act that crowds loved was Martha Jumpjump, who skipped rope on a high wire. (The high wire was really a spider web that had been fixed up so that Martha wouldn't stick to it.)

Then there was the French flea, Henry Ouch, the flea who trained rats. He would get into a cage with four or five rats and have them do all kinds of tricks. If they did not do what he told them to do, he would jump on their backs and bite them.

Aunt Fanny's Flea Circus went around the world, bringing in big crowds and making lots of money. ⭐ But in 1999, Aunt Fanny and the fleas started to fight a lot. The fleas said that Aunt Fanny was hogging all the fame. Aunt Fanny said that she could do what she wanted because she owned the circus. The fleas were mad at Fanny because of the way she acted. After each show, people would come up to Fanny. "Great show, Fanny," they would say. The only thing Fanny did in the show was wave a stick at the fleas. The fleas did the real work.

Also, Aunt Fanny hogged all the money. She kept the poor fleas locked in a little box while she lived in expensive apartments. She fed the fleas dry bread while she ate expensive food. She put thousands of dollars into the bank, but she didn't give the fleas a dime.

One night the fleas made up their minds that things had to change.

"She's treating us like dirt," Carl said. "Are we going to take that?"

"No," all the other fleas agreed. "Things must change."
MORE NEXT TIME

D Number your paper from 1 through 16.

Review Items

1. What do all living things need?
2. What do all living things make?
3. Do all living things grow?

4. Which letter shows where the ground gets warm first?
5. Which letter shows where the ground gets warm last?

The pictures show the same twig in 4 seasons. Write the name of the season for each twig.

6.   7.   8.   9.

10. In the fall, are the leaves on trees **dead** or **alive?**

11. Camels can go for ▮▮▮▮ days without drinking water.

12. How many pounds of water can a 1 thousand-pound camel drink at one time?

13. Which letter shows the felt tip?

14. Which letter shows the ink?

15. Which letter shows the shaft?

16. Write the letter that shows where an eraser would go on a pen.

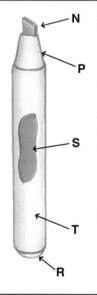

A

1
1. meter
2. yea
3. directions
4. Russia

2
1. <u>greatest</u>
2. <u>minute</u>
3. <u>fancy</u>
4. <u>middle</u>
5. <u>surprise</u>
6. <u>juggle</u>

3
1. second
2. gentlemen
3. tomorrow
4. money
5. scared
6. propped

4
1. week
2. ladies
3. cage
4. hour
5. hoop
6. steel

B # Learning About Time

Names that tell about time tell how long it takes for something to happen. A **week** tells about time. A week is seven days long. So if something will happen a week from now, it will happen seven days from now.

An **hour** is another name that tells about time. If you spent an hour watching TV, you may be able to watch two shows.

A **second** is a name that tells about time. When you count slowly, each number takes about one second.

A **minute** is a name that tells about time. A minute is much smaller than an hour.

Remember, names that tell about time tell how long it takes for something to happen.

C   Facts About Flea Circuses

When we left Aunt Fanny in the last story, the fleas were mad at her. Name three things they were mad about.

The fleas in the story talk, so we know they are make-believe fleas. But there are such things as flea circuses. And these flea circuses do have fleas that put on acts. Here are some facts about real flea circuses:
- Most fleas that are used in flea circuses come from Russia.
- Fleas have been taught to juggle things.
- Fleas have been taught to jump through hoops.
- Some fleas have been taught to pull things that weigh a hundred times more than a flea.

- The first trick a flea must be taught is to walk instead of hop. Fleas like to take a great hop to go from place to place. But they can walk.

After they have been taught to walk, they can be taught to walk on a high wire or to pull a cart.

D The Fleas Surprise Aunt Fanny

The fleas in Aunt Fanny's Flea Circus were tired of the way Aunt Fanny was treating them. They made up their minds to do something about it. Carl spoke for all the fleas. He went to Aunt Fanny and tried to tell her that she would have to change her ways. But she wouldn't even listen to him.

"Please, Carl," she said. "Can't you see I'm late for dinner? Now be a good little flea and go back to your nice little box."

"Go to your dinner," he yelled as loud as he could. "Things will be different tomorrow."

Aunt Fanny was in for a great big surprise the next day. The circus was packed with people. Aunt Fanny picked up her stick and people clapped. "Ladies and gentlemen," she said. "You will see the greatest flea show in the world. The first act is the famous Martha Jumpjump skipping rope on the high wire." Aunt Fanny waved her stick, and Martha went up to the high wire. But she didn't skip rope. She walked to the middle of the wire and fell off. "Booo," the crowd yelled.

The next act was Henry Ouch. He got in the cage with three rats. But he didn't make the rats do tricks. He hopped around the cage while the rats went to sleep. "Boooo," the crowd yelled.

MORE NEXT TIME

E Number your paper from 1 through 12.

Skill Items

Here are titles for different stories:
  a. 100 Ways to Cook Turkey
  b. Why Smoking Will Hurt You
  c. A Funny Story

1. One story tells about reading something that makes you laugh. Write the letter of that title.
2. One story tells about something that is bad for you. Write the letter of that title.
3. One story tells about how to make different meals out of one thing. Write the letter of that title.

Here's a rule: **All the people got mad and booed.**
  4. Tim is a person. So what else do you know about Tim?
  5. Liz is a person. So what else do you know about Liz?

  The fly boasted about escaping from the spider.
  6. What word tells about getting away from something?
  7. What word means **bragged?**

Review Items
  8. Which is longer, a centimeter or an inch?
  9. How many legs does an insect have?
  10. How many legs does a spider have?
  11. How many legs does a flea have?
  12. If a beetle is an insect, what else do you know about a beetle?

14

1	2	3
1. scared	1. south	1. pillow
2. usually	2. measure	2. north
3. fancy	3. crowd	3. meter
4. disappear	4. directions	4. yea
	5. money	5. loop
	6. propped	6. steel

Meters

You're going to read about meters. We use meters to measure how long things are.

A meter is 100 centimeters long.

C **Directions on a Map**

You are going to read about 4 directions: north, south, east, and west. Maps always show:

north on the top.
south on the bottom.
east on this side: ⟶
west on this side: ⟵

If something on a map goes north, it goes this way: ↑
If something on a map goes south, it goes this way: ↓
If something on a map goes this way ⟶ which direction is it going?
If something on a map goes this way ⟵ which direction is it going?

D

Aunt Fanny
Changes Her Ways

The fleas had given Aunt Fanny a surprise. Martha Jumpjump did not do her act. Henry Ouch did not do his act. The crowd did not like the show at all, and Aunt Fanny was getting scared. If the rest of the fleas did not do their acts, Aunt Fanny would have to give money back to the people who paid to see the show.

The next act was Carl Goodscratch. He went up to the top of his 48 centimeter ladder. Then he looked up at Aunt Fanny and said, "Don't you think that you should treat us better? Don't you think that you should give us more money and give us a better place to live?"

Aunt Fanny looked at the little flea. Then she looked at the crowd. They looked mad. "Yes, Carl, yes, yes, yes," she said. ⭐ "Do the dive and I will share everything with you."

"Do you really mean that?" Carl asked.

"Yes, yes, yes, yes, yes," Aunt Fanny said. Her hand was shaking so much that the stick was making a wind.

🌸 So Carl did a dive. People say it was the best dive he ever did. He turned around five times. He made seven loops. And he landed in the water without making any splash at all.

The crowd went wild. "Yea, yea," the people cheered. "What a show!" they shouted.

Now everybody in Aunt Fanny's Flea Circus is happy. Aunt Fanny is happy because the fleas work harder and put on a better show. The fleas are happy because they live in a great big fancy dog house that is a meter high and a meter wide. Any they have 🌸 lots and lots of money.

THE END

E Number your paper from 1 through 14.

Skill Items

Here are titles for different stories:
- a. Jane Goes on a Train
- c. My Dog Likes Cats
- b. The Hot Summer
- d. The Best Meal

1. One story tells about eating good food. Write the letter of that title.
2. One story tells about somebody taking a trip. Write the letter of that title.
3. One story tells about a time of year when people go swimming a lot. Write the letter of that title.
4. One story tells about pets. Write the letter of that title.

Use the words in the box to write complete sentences.

| escaping | covering | visited | remove |
| rough | first | waded | tadpoles | boasted |

5. They ▨▨▨ into the stream to ▨▨▨ ▨▨▨.
6. The fly ▨▨▨ about ▨▨▨ from the spider.

Review Items

7. In the summer, are the leaves on trees **dead** or **alive?**
8. Are those leaves **wet** or **dry?**

9. How many legs does an insect have?
10. How many legs does a spider have?
11. If a bee is an insect, what else do you know about a bee?
12. Where do the fleas in flea circuses usually come from?
13. What's the first thing that fleas must be taught?
14. Write the 4 names that tell about time.
    - centimeter
    - hour
    - inch
    - minute
    - week
    - second
    - meter

A

1
1. Alaska
2. escape
3. rough
4. favorite
5. opposite

2
1. <u>tad</u>poles
2. <u>some</u>times
3. <u>gold</u>fish
4. <u>any</u>body

3
1. boast
2. Goad
3. toaster
4. floating

4
1. <u>mem</u>bers
2. <u>pil</u>low
3. <u>hun</u>ters
4. <u>doll</u>ars

5
1. full-grown
2. family
3. thousands
4. strong
5. disappears
6. covered

6
1. rich
2. shore
3. circus
4. hound
5. front

B Facts About Toads and Frogs

Toads and frogs are members of the same family.
Here are facts about toads and frogs:

- They are born in water, and they live in the water until they are full-grown. Then they move onto the land.

- At first toads and frogs are tadpoles that have no legs.

- Then the tadpoles grow two back legs.

- Then they grow two front legs.

- Then the tail disappears and they are full-grown toads or frogs.

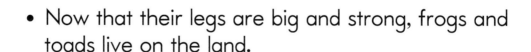

- Now that their legs are big and strong, frogs and toads live on the land.

Remember, they are born in the water and grow up in the water. Then they move to the land.

Goad the Toad

Once there was a toad named Goad. Goad was the biggest toad you have ever seen. Goad was bigger than a baseball. She was even bigger than a toaster.

Goad was not only big. She was smart. She was smarter than a trained seal. Not only was Goad big and smart, Goad was fast. She was faster than a cat chasing a mouse.

Goad lived near a large lake called Four Mile Lake. It was four miles from one end of the lake to the other.

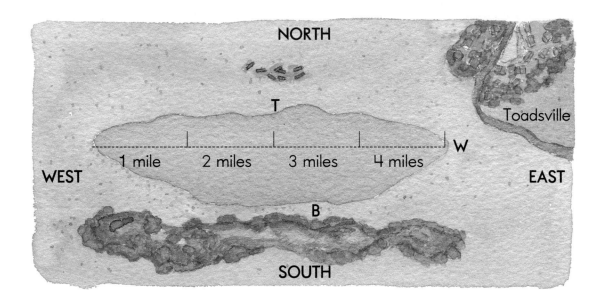

Goad liked to visit places on Four Mile Lake. Sometimes, she would hop over to the logs near the north shore of the lake. Sometimes, she would hop over the hills on the south shore. Sometimes, she would go for a dip near the east shore of the lake.

When Goad was in the water, she ⭐ was not fast. She could not swim as fast as a seal or a goldfish. In fact, she could not swim as fast as a very slow frog. When Goad was in the water, she looked like a floating pillow with two big eyes.

Because Goad was so big, and so fast, and so smart, thousands of hunters went to Four Mile Lake every year to see if they could catch Goad. People from the circus knew that if they had Goad, they could put on a show that would bring thousands of people to the circus. Hunters from zoos knew that people would come from all over to visit any zoo that had a toad like Goad. Some hunters came because they wanted to become rich. Goad was worth thousands of dollars to anybody who could catch her. But nobody was able to catch her.

MORE NEXT TIME

D **Number your paper from 1 through 16.**

Skill Items

Rule: **Frogs have smooth skin.**

1. The rule tells something about any ______.

Rule: **Birds have two feet.**

2. The rule tells something about any ______.
3. Is a robin a bird?
4. Does the rule tell about a robin?
5. Does the rule tell about an ape?

Rule: **The largest mountains were covered with snow.**

6. What's the only thing that rule tells about?

- any mountain
- the largest mountains
- any frog

7. Does the rule tell about Happy Valley?

8. Write the letter of each picture the rule tells about.

 A
 B
 C
 D

Here are titles for different stories:
a. Liz Goes to the Zoo   b. A Pretty New Hat
c. The Green Dog

9. One story tells about someone who went to look at animals. Write the letter of that title.

10. One story tells about a funny-looking animal. Write the letter of that title.

11. One story tells about something you put on your head. Write the letter of that title.

Review Items

12. Which is longer, a centimeter or an inch?

13. Some of the lines in the box are one inch long. Some of the lines are one centimeter long. Write the letter of every line that is one inch long.

14. Write the letter of every line that is one centimeter long.

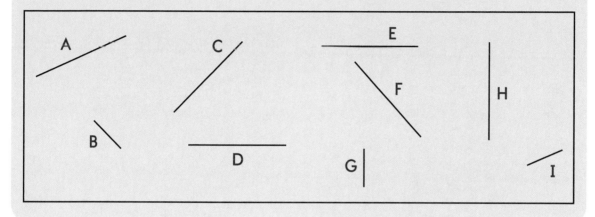

15. Where do the fleas in flea circuses usually come from?

16. What's the first thing that fleas must be taught?

16

A

1
1. covered
2. visited
3. escaped
4. noticed
5. removed
6. stationed

2
1. <u>favorite</u>
2. <u>evening</u>
3. <u>Toads</u>ville
4. <u>hundreds</u>

3
1. warts
2. belly
3. Alaska
4. first
5. opposite

4
1. shovels
2. tongue
3. rough
4. there
5. underground

B More Facts About Toads and Frogs

Toads and frogs are members of the same family. But toads are different from frogs. Here are some facts about how toads and frogs are different:

- Toads have skin that is rough and covered with warts.
- No toads have teeth, but some frogs have teeth.
- The back legs of toads are not as big or strong as the back legs of frogs.

C Goad Uses Her First Trick

Goad lived near Four Mile Lake. Down the road from the lake was a town. The name of that town was Toadsville. It was named Toadsville because so many people who visited the town had come to hunt for a big, smart, fast toad. And in the evening you could find hundreds of people sitting around Toadsville talking about Goad. First they would talk about some of the traps that had been made to catch Goad. Then they would tell how Goad escaped. One of their favorite stories is the one of the great big net.

Five hunters from Alaska had come to Four Mile Lake with a net that was nearly a mile wide. They waited until Goad was on a hill where there were no trees, just some white rocks. Then they flew over the hill in a plane and dropped the great big net over the hill. ⭐ Goad was under the net. The five hunters rushed to the place where Goad had last been seen. But there was no Goad. There was some grass and five large white rocks. The hunters removed the net and began to go over every centimeter of the ground.

Suddenly, one of the hunters noticed that the biggest rock was moving. The biggest rock wasn't a rock at all. It was Goad.

She had moved near the other rocks. Then she had turned over on her back so that her white belly was showing. That belly looked like a white rock. Suddenly, she turned over. "There she is," one of the hunters yelled, but before the others could turn around, Goad hopped down the side of the hill and was gone.

MORE NEXT TIME

D Number your paper from 1 through 16.

Skill Items

Write the word from the box that means the same thing
as the underlined part of each sentence.

weight	measure	leaves	paws
grove	family	hooves	evening

1. The deer ran into the <u>small group of trees</u> to hide.
2. The horse's <u>feet</u> were covered with mud.
3. She used a ruler to <u>see</u> how long the rope was.

4. Look at object A, object B, and object C. Write at
   least **2** ways all 3 objects are the same.

Object A

Object B

Object C

- They are all big.
- They are pink.
- They are not round.
- They are striped.
- They are circles.

The workers propped up the cage with steel bars.

5. What 2 words refer to supporting something?

6. What word names a strong metal?

7. What objects were made of a strong metal?

8. What object was propped up?

Review Items

9. Which is longer, an inch or a centimeter?

10. Some of the lines in the box are one inch long. Some of the lines are one centimeter long. Write the letter of every line that is one centimeter long.

11. Write the letter of every line that is one inch long.

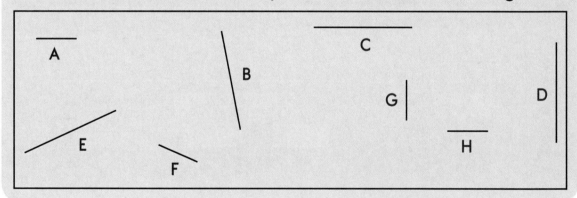

12. Where do the fleas in flea circuses usually come from?

13. What's the first thing that fleas must be taught?

14. What color are the flowers that apple trees make?

15. When do those flowers come out?

16. What grows in each place where there was a flower?

17

A

1
1. famous
2. women
3. breath
4. tongue
5. England
6. silence

2
1. family
2. belly
3. sticky
4. already
5. sixty
6. stubby

3
1. shovels
2. seconds
3. wooden
4. underground
5. halfway

4
1. length
2. blue
3. hundred
4. noticed
5. evening

5
1. distance
2. balloon
3. swallow
4. fourth

B How Far Apart Things Are

Names that tell about length or distance tell how far apart things are. The book your teacher is holding is one foot tall. A ruler is one foot long.

A **mile** is a name that tells how far apart things are. If two things are a mile apart, they are more than 5 thousand feet apart.

A **meter** is a name that tells about length.

A **centimeter** is a name that tells about length.

Remember, miles, feet, meters, centimeters and inches are names that tell about length. They tell how far apart things are.

C How Toads Catch Flies

Toads eat flies. A toad catches flies with its long, long tongue. A toad's tongue is almost as long as the toad. A toad's tongue is covered with sticky goo. The tongue moves so fast that it hits a fly before the fly can move. The fly sticks to the tongue. When the toad pulls its tongue back, the fly comes with it.

The pictures below show a toad's tongue catching a fly.

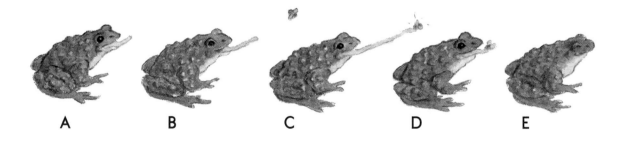

A   B   C   D   E

D Food Traps

The people in Toadsville like to tell stories about Goad and how she escaped from traps. They tell about how she once escaped from the great big net. The people also tell how Goad got away from food traps. One of the hunters' favorite tricks was to make food traps.

PICTURE 1

All food traps work the same way. You put out some food that a toad likes. Maybe you put some blue flies on the ground. My, my, how toads love those blue flies. Then you make a trap that closes on the toad when it goes for the food.

PICTURE 2

PICTURE 3

If the pole tips over, the toad is trapped in the net. Hunters put blue flies at the end of the string. When the toad eats the flies, the string moves ✶ and the pole falls over.

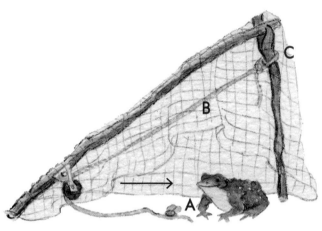

PICTURE 4

Remember, a fly is on the end of the string. So when the fly moves, the string moves. And when the string moves, the pole moves. That pole holds up a net. So when the fly moves, the string moves. And when the string moves, the pole moves. And when the pole moves, the net falls over the toad.

If you believe the stories they tell in the town of Toadsville, Goad has escaped from over five hundred food traps. Not all these stories are true. Goad has really escaped from four hundred food traps, but that's a lot of escaping for one toad. How did she do it? You already know one of her tricks. You'll find out about more of her tricks in the next story.

Skill Items

Rule: **Dogs have four legs.**
1. Write the letter of each object the rule tells about.

A   B   C

D   E   F

Write the word or words from the box that mean the same thing as the underlined part of each sentence.

danger	million	a meter	half	bark	
great	during	ruler	measure	an inch	

2. The <u>tree's covering</u> was full of holes.
3. She went on a <u>wonderful</u> trip.
4. The string was <u>100 centimeters</u> long.

Here are titles for different stories:

a. The Prancing Bear b. The Fly That Couldn't Fly

c. How to Grow Roses

5. One story tells about an insect that was different. Write the letter of that title.
6. One story tells about a large animal that walked on its tiptoes. Write the letter of that title.
7. One story tells about pretty plants. Write the letter of that title.

Use the words in the box to write complete sentences.

steel	third	down	boasted	decided
propped	gulp	escaping	up	

8. The fly ______ about ______ from the spider.
9. The workers ______ ______ the cage with ______ bars.

Story Item

10. People in Toadsville said that Goad had escaped from over five hundred food traps. But Goad had really escaped from ______ food traps.

Review Items

11. Some things happen as tadpoles grow. Write the letter that tells what happens first.

    a. They grow back legs   c. Their tail disappears.
    b. They turn blue.   d. They grow front legs.

12. Write the letter that tells what happens last.

13. Write the letter of each toad in the picture.

 A    B    C

 D   E    F

For items 14 through 17, read each thing that Tina did. Then write the season that tells when she did it.

    • winter   • spring   • summer   • fall

14. Made little apples where each flower was

15. Went to sleep

16. Made big red apples

17. Made leaves and white flowers

A

1
1. decide
2. group
3. binoculars
4. instructions

2
1. tion
2. sion
3. ar
4. al
5. aw

3
1. propped
2. stationed
3. boasted
4. swallowed
5. decided

4
1. steel
2. third
3. sixty
4. breath
5. famous
6. wild

5
1. gulp
2. fourth
3. England
4. blast
5. silence
6. tramping

B   Facts About Moles

Today's story tells something about moles. Here are some facts about moles:

• Moles are animals that spend nearly all their time underground.

- There are different types of moles. Some are big. Some have almost no hair.
- Bigger moles are about the same size as toads.
- Moles cannot see very well. Some types of moles cannot see at all. They even have skin growing over their eyes.
- Moles have legs that work like shovels.

C The Opposite Direction

You're going to learn about things that move the opposite direction. If you move north, the opposite direction is south. If you move up, the opposite direction is down. If you move to the left, the opposite direction is to the right.

What's the opposite direction of north?
What's the opposite direction of down?
What's the opposite of east?
Point to the front of the room.
Now point in the opposite direction.
Point to the floor.
Now point in the opposite direction.

D **Goad's Four Tricks**

Goad has escaped from four hundred food traps. She has four tricks that she uses to escape from those traps. One trick is to make herself look like a rock, the way she did when she escaped from the great net. Her second trick is to dig. You wouldn't think that a toad the size of a pillow could dig very fast, but you have never seen Goad dig. She can dig so fast that worms get mad at her. She can dig faster than a snake. She can even dig faster than a mole. And moles have legs like shovels.

Goad's third trick is to eat the trap. If the food trap is a big wooden box that drops over Goad, that fat toad just smiles to herself and starts eating.

Her fourth trick is to blow the trap away. That's right. She takes in a big breath of air. When she does this, she gets bigger. She gets so big that she looks just like a brown and green and white balloon. ⭐ When she is nearly two times the size of a pillow, she blows. The wind comes out of her mouth so fast that she can blow most traps a hundred meters away. That's how she got away from the famous steel trap.

A man came from England. The man boasted that he had made a trap that could hold any toad. "No toad can eat through this trap," he said. "And no toad can dig under this trap if I put it on hard rock."

And that's just what he did. He propped up the steel trap next to the road, where there was no dirt, just hard rock. Then he put sixty blue flies under the trap.

There is no toad in the world that can stay away from sixty blue flies. So before very long, out popped Goad. Her tongue came out. In one gulp, she had swallowed half of the flies. She was ready for her second gulp, when BONG.

MORE NEXT TIME

E Number your paper from 1 through 12.

Skill Items

Rule: **Tadpoles have a tail.**

1. Milly is a tadpole. So what does the rule tell you about Milly?

    • She has a tail.   • nothing

2. A cat is not a tadpole. So what does the rule tell you about a cat?

    • It has a tail.   • nothing   • It is a tadpole.

Rule: **Cats have eyes.**

3. A robin is not a cat. So what does the rule tell you about a robin?

4. A manx is a cat. So what does the rule tell you about a manx? **Write the complete sentence:** A manx ▓▓▓▓ .

5. Look at object **A** and object **B**. Write 3 ways the objects are the same.

Object A   Object B

① They are both ▨▨▨▨▨.
② They both have ▨▨▨▨.
③ ▨▨▨▨▨▨▨▨▨▨.

Write the word from the box that means the same thing as the underlined part of each sentence.

England	station	famous	steel
breath	bark	Alaska	

6. The <u>tree's covering</u> was burned by the forest fire.

7. This book is <u>well-known</u>.

8. Jill wanted to take a trip to <u>the largest state</u>.

Review Items

9. Write the letters of the 4 names that tell about length. (Remember, those names tell how far apart things are.)

    a. minute   f. week
    b. hour   g. mile
    c. day   h. meter
    d. centimeter   i. year
    e. second   j. inch

10. The names in one box tell about time. Write the letter of that box.

11. The names in one box tell about length. Write the letter of that box.

A	centimeter inch meter mile
B	week year second month minute hour

12. Two things move in opposite directions. One moves toward the front of the room. The other moves toward the ▆▆▆▆.

A

1

tion

sion

1. impre<u>ssion</u>
2. sta<u>tion</u>
3. instruc<u>tion</u>
4. ac<u>tion</u>
5. vaca<u>tion</u>
6. men<u>tion</u>

2

1. <u>tramping</u>
2. <u>weakness</u>
3. <u>stubby</u>
4. <u>problem</u>
5. <u>middle</u>

3

1. women
2. dreams
3. group
4. wild
5. binoculars
6. decided

4

1. wolves
2. holler
3. torch
4. either
5. fifteen
6. motion

B **Binoculars**

Here is a picture of binoculars:

Follow these instructions:
1. Hold your hands so they make circles.

2. Now look through the circles made by your hands.

Looking through binoculars is like looking through the circles made by your hands. But when you look through binoculars, things look very, very big. Things may look ten times as big as they look through the circles made by your hands.

If you see this through the circles made by your hands,

you would see this through a strong pair of binoculars.

If you saw something that looked one centimeter tall through the circles made by your hands, that thing would look ten centimeters tall through strong binoculars.

C How Fast Things Move

Here's the rule: **Names that tell how fast things move have two parts.**

Here's a name that tells how fast things move: **miles per hour.** The two parts are **miles** and **hour.**

Here's another name that tells how fast things move: **meters per second.** The two parts are **meters** and **second.**

Here's a name that does not tell how fast things move: **meters.**

Here's another name that does not tell how fast things move: **hours.**

D The Brown Family Comes to Catch Goad

The famous steel trap came down over Goad. "I told you I could catch her," the man from England boasted as he ran down the road toward the trap. But before he was halfway there, something happened. You could hear the sound of wind. It sounded like air leaking from a tire. Then there was silence. Then there was a great blast of wind, and the famous steel trap went sailing through the air. Goad had used her fourth trick.

Everybody agreed that steel traps couldn't catch Goad, and nets couldn't hold her either. Hundreds of men, women, boys, and girls came tramping over the hills every summer but they couldn't catch her. Even trained hunters and trappers failed. But Goad has one weakness, and if you listen to the groups of people talking in the town of Toadsville, you know what her only weakness is. She can't swim fast. When she's in the water, she's like a great fat lump, with stubby legs that can hardly push her along. At least a thousand people must have said, "If we could just find her when she's swimming, there's no way she could get away." ⭐

❀ That sounds like an easy thing to do, but there is one problem. You first have to find Goad when she is in the water.

There's an old man in the town of Toadsville who shows pictures of Goad swimming in the lake. The old man took the pictures from high above the lake. Everyone who sees the pictures says the same sort of thing. They say, "If I saw that toad swimming in the lake like that, I'd get in a boat and catch her."

Sometimes in the summer you can count hundreds of people stationed around the lake, ❀ ready for action. Some of the people have binoculars. They sit hour after hour, looking through the binoculars. Their great hope is that they will see Goad swimming far from the shore of the lake.

Last summer, a group of wild hunters had the chance that everybody dreams about. They spotted Goad swimming in the middle of the lake. And they were ready for action. These wild hunters were part of the famous Brown family. The Brown family was made up of 40 people. Fifteen of them were on vacation at Four Mile Lake, and they decided to spend all their time looking for Goad.

MORE NEXT TIME

E **Number your paper from 1 through 18.**

Skill Items

Rule: **Trees have leaves.**

1. A maple is a tree. So what else do you know about a maple?
2. A bush is not a tree. So what else do you know about a bush?
3. A weed is not a tree. So what else do you know about a weed?

Story Items

4. What is Goad's only weakness?

- She sleeps too much.
- She has a short tongue.
- She cannot swim fast.

5. People hoped they could be around when Goad was swimming in the lake because ▒▒▒

- she would be easy to hear.
- she would be easy to catch.
- she would be easy to smell.

6. There were 40 people in the Brown family. How many of them were going to try to catch Goad?

- 39   • 15   • 12

Here are Goad's four tricks for escaping from hunters:
- blow the trap away   • look like a rock
- dig   • eat the trap

7. Goad's first trick was to ▒▒▒▒.

8. Goad's second trick was to ▒▒▒▒.

9. Goad's third trick was to ▒▒▒▒.

10. Goad's fourth trick was to ▒▒▒▒.

11. How did Goad get away from the famous steel trap?

Skill Item

12. Look at object **A** and object **B.** Write 3 ways the objects are the same.

Object A

Object B

① They are both ________.
② They both can hold ________.
③ ________.

Review Items

13. Which is longer, a centimeter or a meter?
14. How many centimeters long is a meter?

15. Write the letter of each statement that could not be true.
    a. A toad could fly.
    b. A toad could swim.
    c. A toad was as big as a baseball.
    d. A toad was as big as a house.

16. The names in one box tell about time. Write the letter of that box.

17. The names in one box tell about length. Write the letter of that box.

A | centimeter   inch   meter   mile
B | week   year   second   month   minute   hour

18. Write the letter of each mole in the picture below.

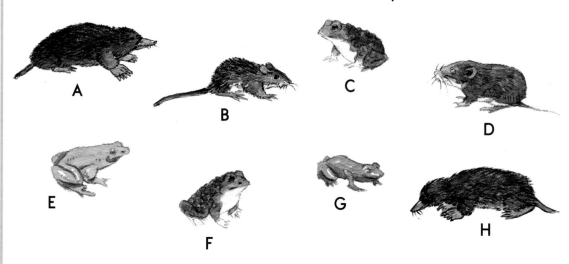

Number your paper from 1 through 22.

1. How many legs does an insect have?

2. How many legs does a spider have?

3. If a beetle is an insect, what else do you know about a beetle?

4. Write the letters of the 4 names that tell about time.

   a. meter   b. second   c. week   d. hour

   e. inch   f. centimeter   g. minute

5. Which is longer, a centimeter or a meter?

6. How many centimeters long is a meter?

---

7. Write the letter of each toad in the picture.

8. Write the letter of each mole in the picture.

A

B

C

D

E

F

---

9. Which animal has smooth skin, a frog or a toad?

10. Which animal can jump farther, a frog or a toad?

11. Do any frogs have teeth?

12. The names in one box tell about time. Write the letter of that box.

13. The names in one box tell about length. Write the letter of that box.

A	centimeter	inch	meter	mile		
B	week	year	second	month	minute	hour

14. An arrow goes from A. Which direction is that arrow going?

15. An arrow goes from B. Which direction is that arrow going?

16. An arrow goes from C. Which direction is that arrow going?

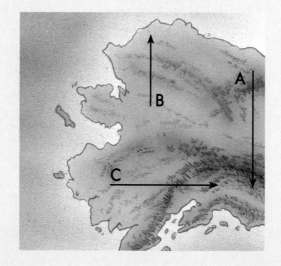

Skill Items

For each item, write the underlined word or words for the sentences in the box below.

> The fly <u>boasted</u> about <u>escaping</u> from the spider.
> The workers <u>propped up</u> the cage with <u>steel</u> bars.

17. What word names a strong metal?
18. What word means **bragged?**
19. What word tells about getting away from something?
20. What 2 words refer to supporting something?

Rule: **Cars use gas.**
21. What's the only thing that rule tells about?
22. Write the letter of each object the rule tells about.

A B C D

━━━━━━ **END OF TEST 2** ━━━━━━

A

1	2	3
1. trouble	1. impression	1. motioned
2. exactly	2. direction	2. stationed
3. engine	3. mention	3. interested
4. ordering	4. question	4. settled
		5. arrived

4	5	6
1. holler	1. toward	1. wolves
2. simple	2. outsmart	2. great
3. smoky	3. grandmother	3. solid
4. torches	4. snapshots	4. twenty
	5. backward	

B # Animals and Fire

You're going to read about how animals act when there is a fire. Here is the rule: **When there is a fire, all animals try to get away from the fire.**

The animals are not interested in hunting for food. The animals are not interested in fighting with other animals. Deer don't like wolves, but when a fire is near, wolves and deer may run side by side. They do not fight or bother each other.

C Smoke and Wind

You're going to read about smoke and wind in today's story. Here's the rule: **The smoke moves in the same direction the wind moves.**

If the wind blows to the north, the smoke moves to the north.

If the wind blows in this direction ⟋, the smoke blows in this direction ⟋.

D The Browns Make Up a Plan

The grandmother in the Brown family gave the impression that she was very mean. She was always ordering the other Browns around. And the other Browns did a lot of yelling. But there's one thing you have to say about the Browns. They were the best hunters that ever came to Toadsville.

When fourteen Browns went running down the hill after something that looked like a great toad, it was something to see. And it was something to hear. That grandmother wasn't far away, yelling at everybody. "Come on, Billy," she'd holler.

Then she'd holler some more. "Run faster. Keep up. Don't look down, Doris. Keep your head up." When Grandmother Brown was on the east side of the lake, the people on the west side of the lake could hear everything she yelled.

After spending three days running after everything that moved, the Browns settled down. They had a plan. They didn't mention anything about what they were going to do, but everybody knew that they had a plan. People would question them. "What are you going to do?" But the Browns didn't answer these questions. The grandmother would usually say, "Stop asking questions. We've got work to do." ⭐

Their plan was simple. First they stationed Browns around the places that Goad liked the most. Everybody knew where these places were. In fact, you can buy little books in the town of Toadsville that show maps of Goad's favorite spots.

The first Brown to spot Goad was Mike. When he saw Goad near the south shore of the lake, he didn't try to rush down and catch her. Instead, he motioned for the other Browns to join him. When the other Browns arrived, they put their plan into action.

They gave Goad the impression that the hills were on fire. The wind was blowing toward the lake. So six Browns lit big smoky torches. These torches made great clouds of smoke. The smoke rolled down the hills toward Goad, who was resting in the grass after eating one bee and sixteen blue flies. Goad was very smart and when she smelled the smoke, she did just what the Browns hoped she would do. She hopped toward the lake. Slowly, the fourteen Browns moved down the hill. Hop, hop. Goad moved closer to the water. As the Browns moved closer,

Goad thought that the fire was coming closer. Hop, hop. Splash.

MORE NEXT TIME

E Number your paper from 1 through 15.

Skill Items

Rule: **Birds have feathers.**

1. A robin is a bird. So what does that tell you about a robin?

2. A tiger is not a bird. So what does the rule tell you about a tiger?

3. A jay is a bird. So what does the rule tell you about a jay?

Use the words in the box to write complete sentences.

trouble	solid	stationed	happened	steel
propped	paddles	opposite	up	

4. The workers ▮▮▮ ▮▮▮ the cage with ▮▮▮ bars.

5. Hunters were ▮▮▮ at ▮▮▮ ends of the field.

Review Items

6. What color are flowers that apple trees make?
7. What grows in each place where there was a flower?

8. What do all living things need?
9. What do all living things make?
10. Do all living things grow?

11. Roots keep a tree from ████.
12. Roots carry ████ to all parts of the tree.
13. When do trees begin to grow?
    - in the winter   - in the spring
14. Trees begin to grow when their roots get ████.
15. In which season is the danger of forest fires greatest?

22

1
1. twenty
2. crazy
3. fuzzy
4. exactly
5. smoky

2
1. boasting
2. roaring
3. ringing
4. screaming
5. believing
6. paddling

3
1. dotted
2. snapshots
3. solid
4. sticking
5. happened
6. upper

4
1. New York
2. trouble
3. impression
4. grown-ups

5
1. engine
2. picnic
3. skip
4. unload

6
1. wrinkle
2. diving
3. movies
4. arrow

B Names That Tell How Fast Things Move

Names that tell how fast things move have two parts. The first part of the name tells about length. The second part tells about time.

Here is a name that tells how fast things move: **centimeters per minute.** The first part of the name is **centimeters.** That part tells about length. The second part of the name is **minute.** That part tells about time.

C How Air Moves an Object

In the story for today, you'll read about how air can move an object. You've seen it happen with balloons. When you fill them with air and let them go, they fly around until they run out of air.

Here's the rule about how the balloon moves: **The balloon moves the opposite direction the air moves.**

Touch the dotted arrow in the picture.

The dotted arrow shows the direction the air moves from the balloon.

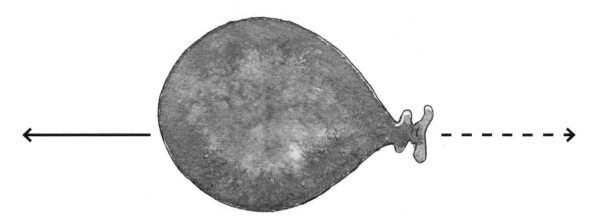

The balloon moves the opposite direction the air moves. The solid arrow shows the direction the balloon will fly through the air.

D Goad in the Water

The Browns had given Goad the impression that a fire was coming down the hill. What really came down the hill were fourteen Browns. The six grown-ups were each carrying a smoky torch. Goad went into the water, thinking that she was getting away from a fire. But she was doing just what the Browns wanted her to do. Her stubby little legs paddled her out into the lake.

When Goad was about twenty meters from the shore, the grandmother motioned to the Browns, and the Browns came roaring down the hill.

The hills were ringing with noise. Every Brown was yelling, "We've got her." But a much louder voice rang above the others. "Mark, move faster." Of course, it was Grandmother Brown, yelling orders to everybody.

It seemed that Goad would never get away from these fourteen screaming Browns. Her little legs were paddling as fast as they could, but she knew that she was in trouble. Browns were running into the water now, diving, splashing, yelling, coming at Goad like fourteen crazy people.

The next part of the story is the part that some people still have trouble believing, because there are still a lot of questions about it. Nobody has movies to show exactly what happened, but a boy from New York who was on vacation took snapshots that show what happened.

The first snapshot shows the Browns splashing toward Goad. In the second snapshot Goad is loading up with air. She looks like a balloon with a lot of air in it. She is almost round, with her stubby little legs sticking out to the sides. In the same picture, there are two or three Browns reaching out for her. One Brown is diving at her, and he looks like he is very close to her.

In the third snapshot, the Browns are standing in the water, pointing up in the air. In the upper corner of the picture, you can see a little fuzzy mark. That's Goad, flying away from the Browns.

MORE NEXT TIME

E Number your paper from 1 through 16.

Skill Items

Write the word from the box that means the same thing as the underlined part of each sentence.

human	remove	horse	motion
boasting	outsmart	escape	expensive

1. That <u>person</u> can run very fast.
2. He was <u>bragging</u> about how fast he is.
3. Goad used her fourth trick to <u>get away</u> from the Browns.

4. Look at object A and object B. Write 2 ways both objects are the same.

Object A   Object B

Review Items

5. Are camels used more in **dry places** or **wet places?**
6. Which animal has smooth skin, a frog or a toad?
7. Which animal can jump farther, a toad or a frog?

Some things happen as tadpoles grow.

8. Write the letter of the first change.

9. Write the letter of the last change.

    a. They grow front legs.   c. They grow back legs.
    b. Their tail disappears.   d. They grow a tongue.

10. The names in one box tell about time. Write the letter of that box.

11. The names in one box tell about length. Write the letter of that box.

A	hour second year minute week month
B	inch meter mile centimeter

12. Which has a tall straight trunk, a forest tree or an apple tree?   • forest tree   • apple tree

13. Which has larger branches, a forest tree or an apple tree?   • forest tree   • apple tree

14. Camel hooves keep camels from sinking in sand. How are camel hooves different from pig hooves?

    • They are harder and longer.
    • They are sharper and smaller.
    • They are wider and flatter.

15. Where do the fleas in flea circuses usually come from?

16. What's the first thing that fleas must be taught?

A

1
1. moist
2. boiled
3. broiled
4. noise

2
1. <u>back</u>ward
2. <u>laughing</u>
3. <u>loud</u>er
4. <u>pic</u>nic
5. <u>load</u>ed

3
1. waded
2. skipped
3. soaked
4. unloaded
5. outsmarted

4
1. strange
2. families
3. smiled
4. crows
5. gathered

5
1. flight attendant
2. wrinkled
3. caught
4. completely
5. worry

B **Facts About** Miles

The story in this lesson will tell about miles. Here are some facts about miles:

- We use miles to tell how far it is between places that are far apart.
- A mile is a little more than five thousand feet.

Look at the map. The numbers on the arrows tell how many miles it is from one place to another place.

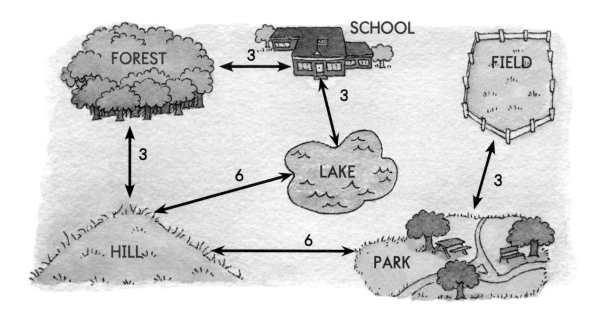

Ⓒ A Big Picnic

The three snapshots of the Browns trying to catch Goad showed Goad in the water, Goad getting bigger, and Goad flying into the air. She had loaded up with air and when the Browns were about to grab her, she unloaded. A great gust of wind came out of her mouth, and she went flying backward. She skipped over the water two times, and then she went straight up into the air. She looked just like a great balloon when you let the air out of it. The Browns just stood there and looked.

One of the Browns said, "Oh nuts," but they seemed to know that Goad had outsmarted them. They didn't run after her. Fourteen Browns stood around in the water watching the great toad land in the weeds about a hundred meters away. Then fourteen soaked Browns waded from the water. They moved slowly.

When they joined the grandmother at the top of the hill, she did something that was very strange. She smiled. Nobody had ever seen her do that before. She had a few missing teeth, but she had a warm smile. It was the kind of old wrinkled smile that makes **you** want to smile. And that's just what happened. ✦ When she smiled, one of the little Browns smiled. Then another Brown smiled, and before you knew it, one of the soaking wet Browns began to laugh. Well, before you knew it, they were all laughing. "That's some toad," one of them yelled, and they all laughed harder.

There's something about seeing fifteen Browns laughing and slapping each other on the back. It makes you start laughing too.

A lot of people had gathered to see the Browns try to catch Goad. The first thing you know, the hills were loaded with people who were laughing. Their cheeks were moist because big tears were running down their cheeks. The sound of the laughing was very loud, but pretty soon, a much louder voice rang above the laughing. "Let's have a picnic and forget about that fat old toad."

And that's just what everybody did. All those people with binoculars and nets who had been watching. All the little kids and the families, and the old people, and dogs and cats and pet crows, and fifteen Browns. They all had a picnic. They ate boiled corn and broiled hot dogs. They did a lot of laughing. And some people say that they could hear somebody else laughing. They say that it sounded like a laughing toad.

THE END

D Number your paper from 1 through 21.

Story Items

1. A boy from New York took three snapshots of Goad getting away from the Browns. What was Goad doing in the second snapshot?

2. What was Goad doing in the third snapshot?

3. Did the Browns catch Goad?

4. What happened right after the grandmother smiled?
   - Everybody else started yelling.
   - Three Browns started crying.
   - Everybody else started laughing.

5. Why were so many other people around the lake?
   - to see the Browns catch Goad
   - to watch the sun set
   - to see the fire

6. Write 2 things that the people ate at the picnic.
   - corn   • cake   • pie   • salad
   - chicken   • hamburgers   • hot dogs

7. Air rushes out of Goad this way ⤤ . Draw an arrow to show which way Goad will move.

8. Air rushes out of Goad this way ⤵ . Draw an arrow to show which way Goad will move.

Skill Items

Here's a rule: **Moles have legs like shovels.**

9. A rat is not a mole. So what does the rule tell you about a rat?

10. Joe is a mole. So what does the rule tell you about Joe?

11. Jan is not a mole. So what does the rule tell you about Jan?

12. Look at object A, object B, and object C. Write **2** ways all 3 objects are the same.

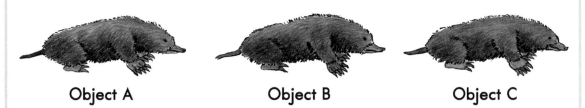

Object A   Object B   Object C

Review Items

13. In which season is the danger of forest fires greatest?

14. Would a pig or a camel sink deeper in sand?

15. A forest fire may burn for ▮▮▮▮.

• weeks   • minutes   • hours

16. Write the letter of each statement that is make-believe.

      a. A dog can jump twenty feet high.
      b. An apple tree can talk.
      c. A forest fire can kill animals.
      d. A frog catches bugs with its tongue.

17. Which arrow shows the way the air will leave Goad's mouth?

18. Which arrow shows the way Goad will move?

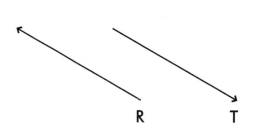

R   T

19. The names in box A tell about ▮▮▮▮.
    - length   - time   - how fast things move
20. The names in box B tell about ▮▮▮▮.
    - length   - time   - how fast things move
21. The names in box C tell about ▮▮▮▮.
    - length   - time   - how fast things move

A	• miles per day • feet per minute • meters per second • meters per hour
B	yard inch meter centimeter mile
C	minute year hour second week month

END OF LESSON 23 INDEPENDENT WORK

SPECIAL PROJECT

Make a large map of Four Mile Lake. Show the directions **north, south, east,** and **west.** Make pictures and labels for the following places:

- ◆ logs
- ◆ hills
- ◆ where the Browns almost caught Goad (Show 6 smoky torches.)
- ◆ Toadsville
- ◆ where you think the Browns had their picnic (Show a picnic table or a hot dog.)

24

A

1
1. mirror
2. CD
3. Nancy
4. spoiled
5. wrong
6. arrows

2
1. completely
2. hanging
3. heavier
4. argued
5. reached
6. smiling

3
1. <u>a</u>head
2. <u>a</u>part
3. <u>a</u>greed
4. <u>any</u>how
5. <u>with</u>in
6. <u>won</u>der

4
1. United States
2. Lisa
3. morning
4. pant
5. Saturday
6. caught

5
1. school
2. worry
3. motioned
4. write
5. bridge
6. thousand

B   More Facts About Miles

Some places are many miles apart.

- If you flew from the east side of the United States to the west side of the United States, you would go about 25 hundred miles.

- If you flew from the north side of the United States to the south side of the United States, you would go about 13 hundred miles.

The map shows the United States.

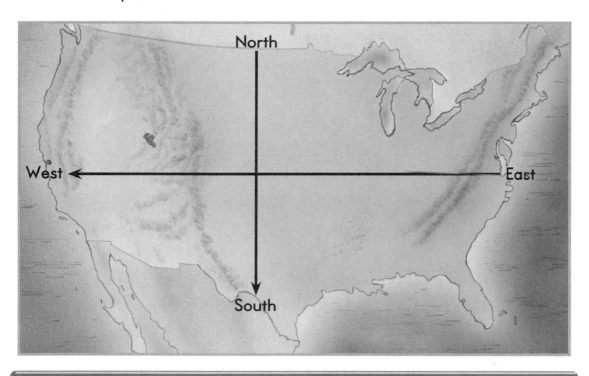

C Jack and Lisa Have a Race

Jack was two years older than his sister Lisa. Jack could do most things better than Lisa. Jack could read better and write better. Jack could lift heavier things than Lisa could lift. And Jack could run faster than Lisa.

But Lisa did something that Jack didn't do. Every morning Lisa got up and ran three miles. While Lisa was running, Jack was still sleeping.

One day Jack and Lisa were on their way to school. Jack said, "You're always running in the morning, but I can still run faster than you. I'll show you. Come on, let's race to the corner."

Before Lisa could say anything, Jack said, "Get ready. Go," and started to run. Lisa ran, too, but she could not keep up with her brother. When Lisa reached the corner, Jack was waiting and smiling, but he was out of breath. He said, "I told you (pant, pant), I could beat you (pant, pant)."

Lisa said, "You are fast in a short race, but I'll bet I can run a mile faster than you can."

Jack said, "That's a joke (pant, pant). I can run a lot faster than you (pant). So I could beat you in a mile (pant)."

Lisa said, "You're already out of breath and we only ran a thousand feet. Remember, a mile is over 5 thousand feet. So your tongue ✦ will be hanging out long before you've run a mile."

Jack said, "That's not (pant) so. I'm faster than you, no matter how far we run."

The children argued some more. Then they agreed to race a mile on Saturday.

✿ On Saturday, Jack and Lisa went to a bike path near the river. They started at a place that was one mile from the big white bridge. Jack said, "By the time you get to the bridge, you'll see me there, resting in the grass."

The race started and Jack was soon far ahead of Lisa. He looked back and smiled. "Come on," he called. "Is that as fast as you can run?"

Lisa did not answer.

By the time Jack could clearly see the white bridge, he was running much slower. Lisa was now right behind him, running quite  a bit faster than he was.

By the time Jack was close enough to read the large signs over the bridge, Lisa was two hundred feet ahead of him. She was pulling away, and he was panting like a sick dog.

Lisa won the race by a thousand feet. After Jack caught his breath and was able to speak without panting, he said to Lisa, "You were right. I can't run a mile as fast as you. So I'll have to start running with you in the mornings."

And that's what he did.

THE END

D Number your paper from 1 through 15.

Skill Items

1. Here's a rule: **The short girls run every morning.**
   Write the letters of the girls who run every morning.

A   B   C   D   E   F

Here are titles for different stories:
   a. Liz Goes to the Zoo
   b. A Pretty New Hat
   c. The Green Dog

2. One story tells about someone who went to look at animals. Write the letter of that title.

3. One story tells about a funny-looking animal. Write the letter of that title.

4. One story tells about something you put on your head. Write the letter of that title.

Review Items

5. How many centimeters long is a meter?

6. Which arrow shows the way the air will leave the jet engines?

7. Which arrow shows the way the jet will move?

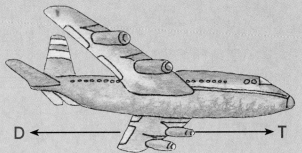

D ⟵   ⟶ T

8. Write the letter of every line that is one inch long.

9. Write the letter of every line that is one centimeter long.

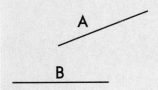

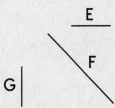
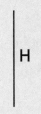

10. Write the letter of each mole.
11. Write the letter of each frog.
12. Write the letter of each toad.

13. Name one way camel hooves are different from pig hooves.

14. Which letter shows where the ground gets warm first?
15. Which letter shows where the ground gets warm last?

1
1. police officer
2. horrible
3. heard
4. badge
5. edge

2
1. tiny
2. silly
3. thirsty
4. Nancy

3
1. <u>door</u>way
2. <u>good</u>bye
3. <u>doll</u>house
4. <u>out</u>fit

4
1. peanut
2. treat
3. screamed
4. greeting

5
1. hurt
2. mirror
3. wearing
4. CD

6
1. spoiled
2. shrunk
3. stamping
4. tight

Telling How Two Things Are Different

You're going to tell how things are different. When you tell how things are different, you must name **both** the objects you're talking about. The things in the picture are object A and object B. When you tell how they are different, you must name object A **and** object B.

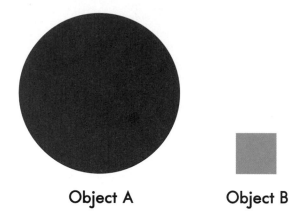

Object A   Object B

Here's a sentence that does **not** tell how they are different: Object A is big. That sentence does not tell about object B.

Here's a right way of telling about that difference: Object A is big, but object B is small.

Remember, to tell one way the objects are different, you have to name **both** objects. Name another way object A and object B are different. Remember to name **both** objects.

C Nancy Wants to Stay Little

Nancy was a spoiled little girl. She liked being little because she could get her way by crying, stamping her feet, turning red in the face, and making lots of noise.

When she acted this way, her mother would say, "If you stop crying, I'll give you a treat." Nancy got lots and lots of treats by crying and acting like a little baby girl.

Then one day something happened. Nancy's dad came home from work. He picked her up and said, "How is my big girl?"

Big girl? Who wants to be a big girl? Nancy knew that if you're a big girl you can't get your way by crying and kicking and stamping and making noise.

After her dad put her down, she went to her room and looked in the mirror. She could see that what her dad said was right. She was getting bigger. The shoes she was wearing were a little tight but when she got these shoes a few months back, they were almost too big for her. Her new striped shirt looked a little small on her.

"Oh nuts," she said in a loud voice. "I don't want to be a big girl." She kicked the mirror and hurt her foot. Then she began to cry and scream and stamp her feet and jump up and down.

That night she had a very bad dream. In her dream she was getting bigger and bigger. When she woke up the ☆ next morning she saw something on her bed. It was a CD. She rubbed her eyes, picked up the CD, and looked at it.

"I don't know how this CD got on my bed," she said to herself. "Maybe it is something from Daddy."

She put the CD in the CD player. A strange voice sang
this song:

"If you hate to be tall, tall, tall,

And you want to be small, small, small,

Just say these words in a good loud voice:

Broil, boil, dump that oil."

Nancy played the CD two times. Then she said, "That's
the worst song in the world."

Later that day she was playing with her friend Sally.
Sally was doing tricks that Nancy couldn't do. Sally
jumped rope. Then she was throwing a ball in the air
and catching it.

Nancy was getting very mad because she could not do
those things. At last she said, "Well, I can do something

you can't do. I can make myself small by saying some words that you don't know."

"No, you can't make yourself small," Sally said.

"Yes, I can," Nancy said. "But I don't feel like doing it now." Nancy didn't really think that she could make herself small, but she wouldn't tell that to Sally.

"You don't know any words that could make you small," Sally said.

Nancy was very mad. "Just listen to this," she said. Then she continued in a loud voice, "Broil, boil, dump that oil."

MORE NEXT TIME

D **Number your paper from 1 through 10.**

1. Which is longer, a centimeter or a meter?

2. How many centimeters long is a meter?

3. The names in one box tell about length. Write the letter of that box.

4. The names in one box tell about time. Write the letter of that box.

A	inch mile meter centimeter
B	month year hour second week minute

5. Which arrow shows the way the air leaves the balloon?

6. Which arrow shows the way the balloon will move?

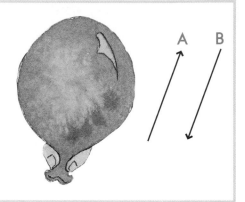

7. Air rushes out of Goad this way ⤺. Draw an arrow to show which way Goad will move.

8. What part of the world is shown on the map?

9. The map shows how far apart some places are. One line shows 13 hundred miles. The other line shows 25 hundred miles. How far is it from **R** to **T**?

10. How far is it from **K** to **M**?

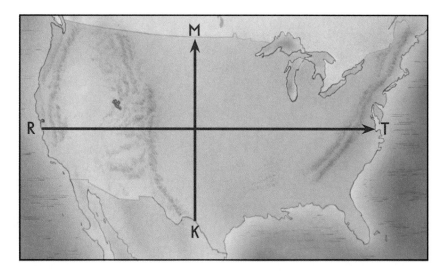

1
1. piece
2. giant
3. brought
4. cabinet
5. although
6. decide

2
1. climb
2. crumb
3. dumb
4. thumb

3
1. police officer
2. flight attendant
3. heard
4. horrible
5. badge
6. peanut

4
1. boom
2. shrunk
3. doorway
4. cookie
5. goodbye
6. beyond

5
1. outfit
2. edge
3. dollhouse
4. bathroom
5. screamed
6. plastic

B

Facts About Ants

The story you'll read today tells about ants. Here are some facts about ants:

- Ants are insects.
  All insects have six legs.
  So ants have six legs.

- Some ants are red and some ants are black.
- Ants are very strong for their size.

Here's a rule: **An ant can carry an object that weighs ten times as much as the ant.** If an ant weighed as much as an elephant, the ant could carry ten elephants.

- Ants are very light. It would take about one hundred ants to weigh as much as a peanut.

C A Green Man Visits Nancy

Nancy had just said some words that she had heard on a CD. All at once, the world began to spin around and around. Then Sally started to grow bigger, bigger, and bigger. Sally wasn't the only thing that began to grow. The jump rope that Sally was holding began to get larger.

Sally's voice boomed out, "Oh, what's wrong? Oh, what's wrong?" The world was still turning and spinning and things were getting larger and larger. Now Nancy was no taller than the grass next to the sidewalk.

Sally was looking down at Nancy. "Oh, Nancy, what's wrong? You're just a little tiny thing. I'll get somebody to help."

Sally dropped her jump rope and ran away. Each step that Sally took shook the ground. Nancy looked around. She was too afraid to cry. And besides, it wouldn't do any good. There was nobody around to treat her like a baby.

An ant came running along the sidewalk. When Nancy looked at the size of the ant, she knew that she had grown even smaller. To her, that ant was the size of a horse. The ant looked very mean—with its round shiny head and six legs running.

Nancy was so frightened that she screamed, but her voice did not sound like it should. Her voice had become smaller as she ⭐ grew smaller. Now her voice was so small that it sounded like a little squeak. You couldn't hear her voice five meters away. "Squeak," she screamed.

At that moment, a voice behind her said, "Go away, ant." The ant turned and ran off down the sidewalk. Nancy turned around and saw a little green man no taller than she was. "Greetings," the man said. "I am the one who made the CD."

"Hello," Nancy said slowly. Then she said, "Why did you give me that funny CD?"

The little man said, "You didn't want anybody to call you a big girl. And you got your wish. Nobody would call a tiny thing like you a big girl."

"I guess you're right," Nancy said. "But I really didn't want to be this little. I'm so little now that . . . "

"Now, now," the green man said. "You should be very, very happy. Even if you grow two times the size you are now, you'll be smaller than a blue fly. Even if you grow twenty times the size you are now, you'll be smaller than a mouse. So you should be very glad."

"Well, I don't . . . "

"I'll walk to your house with you and then I must go," the green man said. "Don't stay outside too long. There are cats and rats and loads of toads that love to eat things your size."

MORE NEXT TIME

D **Number your paper from 1 through 13.**

Skill Items

Here's a rule: **All the green men are small.**

1. Lee is a green man. So what does the rule tell you about Lee?
2. Jack is not a green man. So what does the rule tell you about Jack?
3. Fred is not a green man. So what does the rule tell you about Fred?

Review Items

4. Write the letters of the 4 names that tell about time.
    a. meter
    b. hour
    c. second
    d. centimeter
    e. minute
    f. week
    g. inch

5. Which animal can jump farther, a toad or a frog?

6. Which animal has smooth skin, a toad or a frog?

7. Do any frogs have teeth?

8. Write the letters of the 4 names that tell about length.
    a. week
    b. hour
    c. second
    d. mile
    e. day
    f. minute
    g. centimeter
    h. year
    i. meter
    j. inch

9. When wouldn't a fox bother a rabbit?
    • during spring   • during a fire   • at night

10. What part of the world is shown on the map?

The map shows how far apart some places are. One line shows 13 hundred miles. The other line shows 25 hundred miles.

11. How far is it from **A** to **B**?

12. How far is it from **C** to **D**?

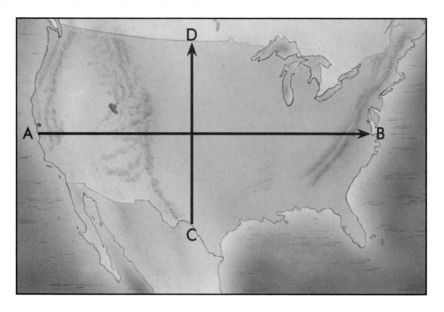

13. A mile is a little more than ▮▮▮▮ feet.

- 5 hundred • 1 thousand • 5 thousand

1
1. decide
2. cabinet
3. bathroom
4. cookie

2
1. flight attendant
2. police officer
3. plastic
4. badge
5. horrible

3
1. although
2. brought
3. bedroom
4. pieces
5. grain

4
1. dollhouse
2. outfit
3. shrunk
4. beyond
5. crumb

Nancy Is Still Tiny

The green man walked with Nancy into her house. They didn't open the door. They walked right through the crack at the bottom of the door. Then Nancy and the green man walked to Nancy's room. As soon as they were inside the room, the green man said, "Goodbye," and he left.

So there was Nancy, all alone in her room. When she had been bigger, she loved to spend time in her room.

She had her dolls, her dollhouse, and her toy trains. She had a TV set, and she had CDs. Things were not the same now that she was so small.

Nancy couldn't play with her dolls because they were at least one hundred times bigger than she was. In fact, the dollhouse was so big that Nancy almost got lost walking around inside it. She tried to turn on her TV, but she couldn't make the button move. That button was five times as big as she was.

Somehow, she made the CD player work. It already had a CD in it, and when she turned on the player, a great voice came from the player. The voice was so loud that it knocked Nancy down. "If you hate to be tall, tall, tall," the voice boomed. Nancy held her hands over her ears and tried to get away from the horrible noise. It seemed as if a long time passed before the CD ended, but suddenly it was quiet in the room again.

Nancy's head hurt and she ⭐ felt very tired. She went back into the dollhouse and found a bed. The bed was far too big for Nancy but she curled up in a corner of the bed and took a nap.

She slept for about an hour and when she woke up, she heard voices in the room. One voice was her mother's. The other voice belonged to a man who looked bigger than three mountains. He was dressed in a dark blue outfit, and he wore a shiny badge. Nancy's mother was crying.

Nancy's mother said, "I don't know where she went. We've looked all over for her, but nobody's seen her."

The police officer said, "Now, let me make sure I understand this. The last time Nancy was seen she was playing with Sally Allen. Is that right?"

Nancy's mother said, "That's right, she was playing with Sally."

The police officer said, "And Sally Allen claims that Nancy shrunk up until she was less than one centimeter tall."

A large tear fell down and almost hit Nancy. The tear was bigger than she was. "I don't know what made Sally make up such a crazy story," Nancy's mother said. "But all I know is that my dear little Nancy is gone and I miss her. I love her very much."

"Here I am, Mom," Nancy shouted from the doorway of her dollhouse. But her voice was so small that it sounded like a tiny, tiny squeak that wasn't as loud as the sound a new shoe makes when it squeaks.

MORE NEXT TIME

C Number your paper from 1 through 11.

Skill Items

> **He motioned to the flight attendant ahead of him.**
>
> 1. One word tells about somebody using his hands to tell a person what to do. What's that word?
> 2. Which two words refer to a person who takes care of passengers on a plane?
> 3. Which word means **in front?**

Review Items

4. What do all living things need?
5. What do all living things make?
6. Do all living things grow?

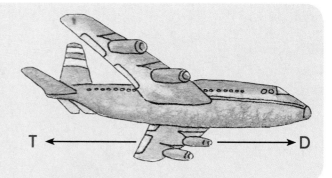

7. Which arrow shows the way the air will leave the jet engines?
8. Which arrow shows the way the jet will move?

9. A mile is a little more than ▮▮▮▮ feet.
   • 1 thousand   • 5 hundred   • 5 thousand

10. If an ant weighed as much as a desk, the ant could carry an object as heavy as ▮▮▮.

11. How many ants would it take to weigh as much as a peanut?

1
1. probably
2. tough
3. sweater
4. learn
5. umbrella

2
1. closely
2. wobbled
3. easily
4. stretched
5. building
6. decided

3
1. catch your breath
2. hoist
3. crumb
4. although
5. bedroom
6. traffic

4
1. stale
2. cabinet
3. piece
4. grain
5. squirrel
6. scary

5
1. bathroom
2. cookie
3. beyond
4. strider
5. tube
6. dew

Sugar Shines

The story you'll read today talks about how sugar shines. A grain of sugar is much smaller than an ant. It is no bigger than a grain of sand.

The picture shows what a grain of sugar would look like if it were big. The grain in the picture has sharp corners. Each side is very smooth. The sugar looks like glass. And the sugar shines like glass.

Nancy Finds Something to Eat

Nancy was shouting and waving her arms, but her mother and the police officer didn't see her as they walked from the room. Although Nancy ran as fast as her tiny legs could move, she couldn't keep up with them. By the time she reached the doorway to her bedroom, she was tired. For her mother and the police officer, the walk to the doorway took only a few steps. But for Nancy it was a long, long run.

Nancy decided not to follow her mother beyond the bedroom door. Nancy didn't want to get lost. So she stood there trying to catch her breath.

Then she walked slowly back toward her dollhouse. On the way, she looked at all the bits and pieces of things that were stuck in the carpet. Between those giant ropes of blue and green were giant pieces of dirt and giant crumbs. One crumb was the size of a bucket next to Nancy. It was a cookie crumb. "I wonder how long it's been here," Nancy said to herself. "I wonder if it's stale." She felt silly for the thought that was going through her head. She was thinking, "If that cookie crumb is any good, I'll eat the whole thing. It will be like eating the world's biggest cookie."

So she bent over and sniffed the cookie crumb. Then she tapped it with her fist. Then she broke off a little piece. That piece sparkled with shiny sugar. Slowly, she brought the piece of cookie to her mouth and took a tiny bite from it. "Not bad," she said to herself. "Not bad at all." She took a big bite and another. With two hands she lifted up the whole crumb and began to eat it. She ate about half of it, and then she stopped. She wasn't hungry any more.

"I need a glass of water," she said to herself. She didn't really need a glass of water. She needed much less than a drop of water. But how do you get water when you're smaller than a fly? How do you get water if you can't reach something as high as a sink? "Water," Nancy said to herself. "I must find water."

MORE NEXT TIME

D Number your paper from 1 through 17.

Skill Items

Use the words in the box to write complete sentences.

thrown   changed   stationed   motioned
opposite   wonder   flight   after   ahead

1. Hunters were ▨▨▨ at ▨▨▨ ends of the field.
2. He ▨▨▨ to the ▨▨▨ attendant ▨▨▨ of him.

Review Items

3. In which season is the danger of forest fires greatest?

4. Camels can go for ▨▨▨ days without drinking water.

5. How many pounds of water can a 1 thousand-pound camel drink at one time?

6. Which is longer, an inch or a centimeter?

7. How many legs does an insect have?

8. How many legs does a flea have?

9. If a fly is an insect, what else do you know about a fly?

10. Which is longer, a centimeter or a meter?

11. How many centimeters long is a meter?

12. A toad catches flies with its ▮▮▮▮▮.

   • tongue   • feet   • legs

13. Why do flies stick to a toad's tongue?
   • because the tongue is sticky
   • because the tongue is dirty
   • because the tongue is dry

14. If an ant weighed as much as a dog, the ant could carry an object as heavy as ▮▮▮▮▮.

15. When do trees begin to grow?

   • in the winter   • in the spring

16. Trees begin to grow when their roots get ▮▮▮▮▮.

17. Camel hooves keep camels from sinking in sand. How are camel hooves different from pig hooves?
   • They are harder and longer.
   • They are sharper and smaller.
   • They are wider and flatter.

1
1. finally
2. easily
3. closely
4. slowly
5. probably
6. early

2
1. building
2. wobbled
3. stretched
4. thirsty
5. weighs
6. moving

3
1. hoist
2. tough
3. sweater
4. squirrel
5. dew
6. forty

4
1. cover
2. discover
3. discovered
4. finished
5. umbrella

5
1. water strider
2. lawn
3. learn
4. tube
5. traffic

Water Has a Skin

The next story tells about the skin that water has. You can see how that skin works by filling a small tube with water. Here's a picture of what you will see.

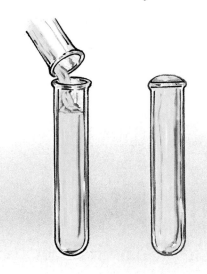

- The top of the water is not flat.
- The skin bends up in the middle.

C

Facts About Dew

The story you'll read today talks about dew. The drops of water that you see on grass and cars early in the morning is called dew.

Here are some facts about dew:
- Dew forms at night.
- Dew forms when the air gets cooler.
- Dew disappears in the morning when the air warms up.

D Nancy Tries to Get Some Water

✿ If Nancy knew more about very small things, she wouldn't have been so afraid of climbing to high places to find water. Here's the rule: **If tiny animals fall from high places, they don't get hurt.** If we dropped an ant from a high airplane, the ant would not be hurt at all when it landed on the ground. A mouse wouldn't be hurt either. A squirrel wouldn't be badly hurt. A dog would probably be killed. And you can imagine what would happen to an elephant.

Nancy was thirsty, so thirsty that she wanted to yell and scream and ✿ stamp her feet like a baby.

Nancy knew that it wouldn't do any good to act like a baby. So she made up her mind to start thinking. She was pretty smart. She said to herself, "If it were early morning, I could go out and drink dew from the lawn." But the grass was not moist with dew, and Nancy couldn't wait until morning.

So she went to the bathroom, looking for water. She had walked from her bedroom to the bathroom hundreds of times before, but this time it wasn't a walk. It was a long, long trip. She finally arrived in the bathroom. She walked around as ★ she made up a plan for getting water. Here's that plan: She would climb up the corner strip of the cabinet. That strip was made of rough wood and it was easy to grip. It went straight to the top of the cabinet.

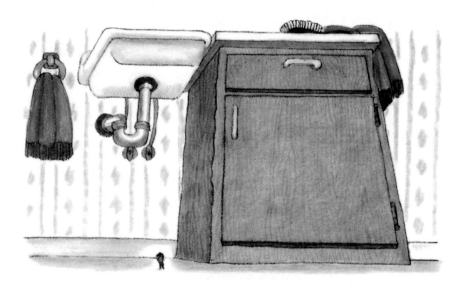

Nancy didn't know what kind of problem would meet her at the top of the cabinet. But first she had to get to the top. So up she went. She hoisted herself up one centimeter, two centimeters. Slowly, up. Then she began moving faster and faster. "This isn't too hard," she said to herself. When she was almost at the top, she reached a spot where the strip was moist with oil. And she slipped. She fell all the way to the floor.

The fall scared her. She landed on her back. For a moment she didn't move. Then she got up slowly, testing her arms and legs to make sure that they weren't hurt. She had fallen from something that was a hundred times taller than she was, but she wasn't hurt. She wasn't hurt at all, not one broken bone. Not one scratch. Not even an ouch.

"I don't know what's happening," Nancy said to herself. "But I'm not afraid to try climbing that cabinet again."

This time she got to the top.

MORE NEXT TIME

E **Number your paper from 1 through 14.**

Skill Items

Here's a rule: **Horses eat grass.**

1. A cow is not a horse. So what does the rule tell you about a cow?

2. Jake is not a horse. So what does the rule tell you about Jake?

3. Meg is a horse. So what does the rule tell you about Meg?

Review Items

4. Roots keep a tree from ▬▬.

5. Roots carry ▬▬ to all parts of the tree.

6. Camels can go for ▬▬ days without drinking water.

7. How many pounds of water can a 1 thousand-pound camel drink at one time?

Some of the lines in the box are one inch long and some are one centimeter long.

8. Write the letter of every line that is one centimeter long.

9. Write the letter of every line that is one inch long.

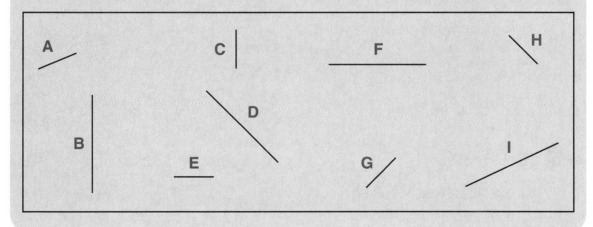

10. What part of the world is shown on the map?

The map shows how far apart some places are. One line shows 13 hundred miles. The other line shows 25 hundred miles.

11. How far is it from **F** to **G**?

12. How far is it from **H** to **K**?

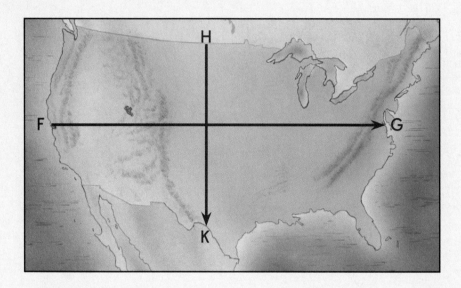

13. If a grain of sugar were very big, it would look like a box made of ▮▮▮▮.

14. What kind of corners does a grain of sugar have?

Number your paper from 1 through 25.

1. When wouldn't a fox bother a rabbit?

- during spring
- at night
- during a fire

Here are names that tell how fast things move.

2. meters per minute
4. centimeters per month

3. inches per second
5. miles per hour

Write the part of each name that tells about time.

6. Which arrow shows the way the air will leave the jet engines?

7. Which arrow shows the way the jet will move?

E ← → D

Let's say this line ⟷ on the map is 3 miles long.
And this line ⟵———⟶ is 6 miles long.

8. Write the letter of a line on the map that is 3 miles long.

9. Write the letter of a line on the map that is 6 miles long.

10. How far is it from the hill to the lake?

11. How far is it from the forest to the school?

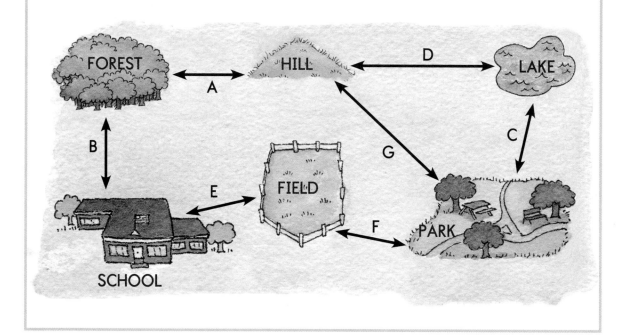

12. A mile is a little more than [blank] feet.

13. What part of the world is shown on the map?

One line on the map is 13 hundred miles long. The other line is 25 hundred miles long.

14. How far is it from **A** to **B**?

15. How far is it from **P** to **T**?

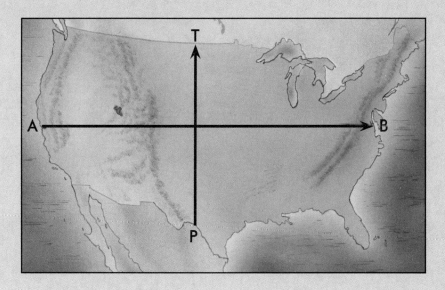

16. If an ant weighed as much as a bird, the ant could carry an object as heavy as ▓▓▓▓▓.

17. You can see drops of water on grass early in the morning. What are those drops called?

18. **Finish the rule.** If tiny animals fall from high places, they don't ▓▓▓▓▓.

Skill Items

Here's a rule: **Dogs pant after they run fast.**

19. Fido is a dog. So what does the rule tell you about Fido?

20. Spot is not a dog. So what does the rule tell you about Spot?

For each item, write the underlined word or words from the sentences in the box.

Hunters were <u>stationed</u> at <u>opposite</u> ends of the field. He <u>motioned</u> to the <u>flight attendant</u> <u>ahead</u> of him.

21. What underlining tells about a person who takes care of passengers on a plane?

22. What underlining tells they were not at the same end of the field?

23. What underlining means **in front?**

24. What underlining tells about something you could do with your hands?

25. What underlining tells that the hunters had to stay where they were placed?

END OF TEST 3

1
1. unit
2. search
3. complain
4. refrigerator
5. supposed
6. decision
7. couple

2
1. stretched
2. discovered
3. weighed
4. finished
5. learned

3
1. <u>house</u>fly
2. <u>bee</u>tles
3. <u>dark</u>ness
4. <u>um</u>brella

4
1. easily
2. strider
3. scary
4. wondering
5. sweater

5
1. gram
2. fright
3. frighten
4. frightened
5. tough
6. scale

B   More About the Skin That Water Has

When we fill a tube with water, you can see that the water has a skin. You can use a dish of water and a hair to show that water has a skin.

First you can float a hair on water. If you're careful, the hair won't even get wet. It will just rest on the skin of the water.

Hair A in the picture is resting on the water.

Look at hair B. The end of that hair is pushed down through the skin of the water. As the hair goes down, the skin of the water bends down around the hair. Look at the skin around hair B.

The end of hair C is under the water. But hair C is moving up. When the hair moves up slowly, the skin hangs onto the hair and bends up. Remember, when the hair goes up, the skin bends up. When the hair goes down, the skin bends down.

C Nancy Gets Some Water

Nancy had climbed to the top of the cabinet. She was ready to have a nice drink of water. Next to the sink there were lots of drops of water. Some drops were bigger than she was. Some drops were about the size of an open umbrella top. She rushed over to them.

Nancy didn't know much about water drops. Here's the rule: **Water drops have a skin that goes all the way around them.** That skin is tough. If you are at a pond, you may see little insects called water striders that walk right on top of the water. They are walking on the skin of the water.

If you look closely, you can see that the legs of water striders make little dents in the water but their legs do not go into the water. The legs just bend the skin of the water down without going through the skin.

Nancy had seen water striders, but she didn't think about how tough the skin of water must be if you are very small. She ran over to one drop of water. The drop of water came up to her knees. Then she bent over and touched the water drop with her hands. It felt like a water

balloon. When she pushed, the skin moved in. But her hands didn't go through the skin. ⭐ "How do insects drink water?" she thought for an instant. Then she got back to her problem. "How am I going to drink?"

"I'll just hit it harder," she thought. She made a fist, wound up and swung as hard as she could swing. Her fist went right through the skin of the drop. Her hand was wet and her arm was wet. She pulled her hand back, but it didn't come out easily. It stuck at the wrist.

She pulled and tugged, and the skin of the water stretched out. Finally, **pop.** Her hand came out, and the skin of the drop wobbled back into its round shape.

Nancy thought about the best way of getting water from the drop. At last, she backed up a few steps, put her head down, and charged the drop of water. Her head hit the water drop and **pop.** Her head went through the skin.

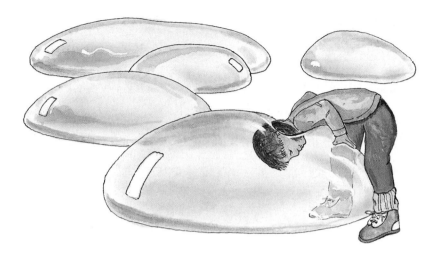

She drank quickly, trying not to get water in her nose. Then she pulled her head back. The skin of the water tugged at her neck. The water pulled at her neck the way a tight sweater pulls on your neck when you try to take it off. Nancy pulled hard, and **pop.** Her head came out of the drop.

"That was scary," she said out loud.

MORE NEXT TIME

D Number your paper from 1 through 22.

Story Items

1. Some drops of water were ▓▓▓ than Nancy.
   - bigger • older • hotter

2. When Nancy first touched the water drop, did her hand get wet?

3. What did Nancy have to do to get her hand inside the water drop?

- look at the drop
- hit the drop
- touch the drop

4. Did Nancy get her head inside the water drop?

5. What happened when Nancy tried to pull her head back out of the water drop?

- It got smaller.
- It got stuck.
- It got wet.

6. Write the letters of the water striders.

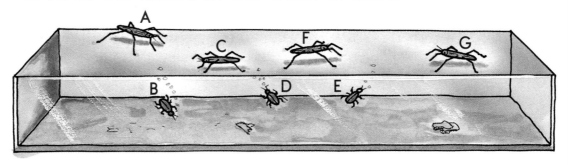

List the three things that Nancy has learned about being very small.

7. Small animals have a voice that is ░░░░░.

8. Small animals don't get hurt when they ░░░░░.

9. Water has a ░░░░░.

10. Is a water strider an insect?

11. How many legs does a water strider have?

12. How many legs does an ant have?

13. How many legs does a spider have?

14. How many legs does a flea have?

15. How many legs does a cat have?

Skill Items

16. Write one way that tells how both objects are the same.

17. Write 2 ways that tell how object A is different from object B.

Object A

Object B

Write the word from the box that means the same thing as the underlined part of each sentence.

heard	hoisted	long	sale
lawn	silly	boomed	stale

18. The cake was <u>old and not very good to eat</u>.

19. The <u>grass</u> was wet after the rain.

20. They <u>lifted</u> the TV onto the truck.

Review Items

21. The names in one box tell about time. Write the letter of that box.

22. The names in one box tell about length. Write the letter of that box.

A	centimeter	inch	meter	mile		
B	week	year	second	month	minute	hour

1
1. discovered
2. frightened
3. wondered
4. finished
5. complained
6. learned
7. supposed

2
1. <u>house</u>flies
2. <u>for</u>ever
3. <u>base</u>ball
4. <u>foot</u>ball

3
1. stale
2. grams
3. search
4. moving
5. traffic
6. forty
7. couple

4
1. decision
2. refrigerator
3. weighs
4. dining
5. chunk
6. toast

5
1. hoist
2. lawn
3. reply
4. replied
5. thirty
6. unit

Grams

In some stories, you've read about things that do not weigh very much. When we weigh very small things, the unit we use is grams.

Here's a rule about grams: **All grams are the same weight.**

If you had a block of water that was one centimeter on all sides, that block would weigh one gram.

A pencil weighs more than a gram. A long pencil weighs about five grams. A short pencil weighs about two grams.

C Nancy Is Hungry Again

Nancy found out three things about being very small. She found out that small things have very high voices. She also discovered that very small things do not hurt themselves when they fall from high places. The third thing she discovered was that a drop of water is very different to someone who is quite small.

During her first night of being small, Nancy found out a fourth fact about being small. Here's the rule: **The food that a very small animal eats each day weighs more than the animal.**

Let's say a small animal weighs one gram. The food that the animal eats each day weighs more than one gram. The food that bigger animals eat each day does not weigh as much as the animals. An elephant may eat two hundred pounds of food each day, but the elephant may weigh more than a thousand pounds. An adult human may eat five pounds of food each day, but the adult weighs much more than five pounds. A large dog may eat three pounds of food every day but the dog may weigh more than 80 pounds.

Nancy learned this rule during the first night that she was very small. She woke up in the middle of the night. She was very hungry. So she got up from her dollhouse bed and went looking for another chunk of cookie that was on her rug. She found one and ate it. Then she felt thirsty, so she went back to the bathroom, climbed to the top of the cabinet, and drank from a drop of water.

"That's scary," she said when she finished.

She went back to bed in her dollhouse, but before the sun came up, she woke up again. She was hungry. The cookie crumbs were gone so she couldn't eat cookie crumbs. She tried to forget about how hungry she was. She knew that she had already eaten a chunk of cookie that weighed almost as much as she did. She wondered, "How can I still be hungry?"

The feeling of hunger did not go away. After a few minutes, she got out of bed. "Oh nuts," she said. "I'm going to have to go hunting for food."
MORE NEXT TIME

D Number your paper from 1 through 14.

Skill Items

1. Write one way that tells how both objects are the same.
2. Write 2 ways that tell how object A is different from object B.

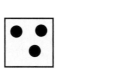

Object A

                    Object B

The traffic was moving 27 miles per hour.

3. How fast was the traffic moving?
4. If the traffic was moving 27 miles per hour, **how far** would a car go in one hour?
5. What word in the sentence refers to all the cars and trucks that were moving on the street?
6. What word means **each**?

Review Items

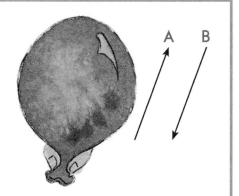

7. Which arrow shows the way the air leaves the balloon?

8. Which arrow shows the way the balloon will move?

9. Write the letters of the 4 names that tell about length.

a. minute   d. centimeter   g. mile   i. year
b. hour   e. second   h. meter   j. inch
c. day   f. week

Look at the skin around each hair.
- Make an arrow like this ↑ if the hair is moving up.
- Make an arrow like this ↓ if the hair is moving down.

10.   11.   12.   13.   14.

33

A

1
1. instead
2. couple
3. expression
4. important

2
1. soundly
2. moments
3. wondering
4. frightened
5. baseballs

3
1. forever
2. refrigerator
3. footballs
4. decision
5. answered

4
1. chunk
2. search
3. scale
4. cherry
5. toast

5
1. yourself
2. whirl
3. swirl
4. learned
5. dining

B **More About Grams**

You learned about grams. You know that grams are used to weigh some kinds of things.

You know how much water it takes to weigh one gram. You know how much a long pencil weighs. You know how much a short pencil weighs.

Here are some facts about how much other things weigh. A big cherry weighs about ten grams. An apple weighs about two hundred grams.

Most insects weigh much less than a gram. Even a very big spider like the spider in the picture weighs less than a gram.

It would take about one hundred ants to weigh one gram.

It would take about thirty houseflies to weigh one gram.

It would take about two hundred fleas from Russia to weigh one gram.

The picture below shows how much a big beetle weighs. How many grams of water are on the scale? So how much weight is on the side of the scale with the beetle?

C Nancy Finds Some More Food

Nancy went toward the kitchen. The walk seemed to take forever. The house was dark and Nancy couldn't see well, so she felt the walls and walked slowly toward the kitchen. When she was in the dining room, she could hear the sound of the refrigerator. In fact, she could feel the refrigerator. It shook the floor.

Finally, Nancy reached the kitchen. By now, she was so hungry that she wanted to scream and cry and kick and roll around on the floor like a baby. But she didn't do any of those things because she knew that acting like a baby wouldn't do any good. So she opened her eyes wide and tried to look for scraps of food.

Near the refrigerator, she found something. She bent over and sniffed it. She wasn't sure what it was, but it smelled bad. "I'm not that hungry," she said. "I'll bet that chunk of food has been on the floor for a week."

Nancy walked nearly all the way around the kitchen, but she couldn't find any other food. "I'll bet there's food on the counter," she said to herself.

Up she went, without feeling frightened. She reached the top and began to ☆ search the counter.

She smelled it before she saw it—toast. She followed her nose. In the darkness, she could just see the toast. Three pieces of toast were piled on a plate. To Nancy, the pile of toast looked like a giant ten-story building.

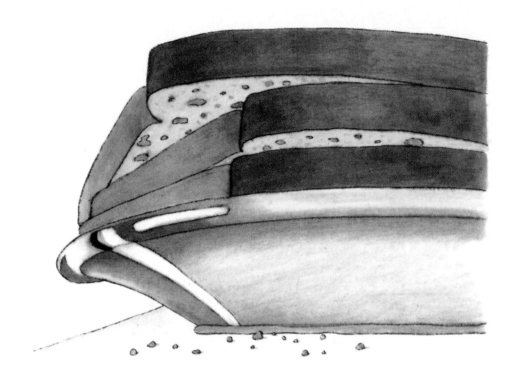

Nancy was wondering how to climb onto the plate so that she could reach the toast. But when she started to walk around the plate, she found crumbs all over the counter. There were crumbs that seemed as big as baseballs and crumbs as big as footballs. There was even one crumb that was the size of a chair.

Nancy picked up a crumb that was the size of a football. She ate it with a loud, "Chomp, chomp, chomp."

When Nancy had been full-sized, she hated toast. She complained when her mother served it. "Oh, not that stuff," she used to say. "I hate toast."

Now that she was small and hungry all the time, she didn't hate toast. In fact, that crumb of toast tasted so good that she ate another piece the size of a football.

Nancy weighed much less than a gram. In one day, she had eaten food that weighed a gram.

MORE NEXT TIME

Number your paper from 1 through 14.

1. Does a housefly weigh **more than a gram** or **less than a gram?**

2. Does a glass of water weigh **more than a gram** or **less than a gram?**

3. How many ants would it take to weigh one gram?

4. How many grams are on the left side of the scale?

5. So how much weight is on the side of the scale with the water striders?

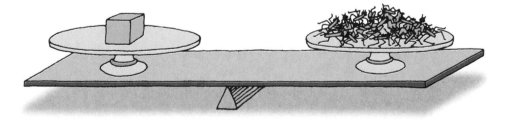

6. Which weighs more, one gram or one water strider?

Skill Items

Use the words in the box to write complete sentences.

stationed	traffic	after	ahead	opposite
per	motioned	wonder	attendant	

7. He ▆▆▆▆ to the flight ▆▆▆▆ ▆▆▆▆ of him.
8. The ▆▆▆▆ was moving forty miles ▆▆▆▆ hour.

Review Items

9. Write the letters of the 4 names that tell about time.

    a. week   b. inch   c. centimeter   d. second

        e. minute   f. meter   g. hour

10. If a grain of sugar were very big, it would look like a box made of ▆▆▆▆.

11. What kind of corners does a grain of sugar have?

12. When we weigh very small things, the unit we use is ▆▆▆▆.

13. The food that 3 of the animals eat each day weighs as much as those animals. Write the letters of those animals.

14. The food that 4 of the animals eat each day does not weigh as much as those animals. Write the letters of those animals.

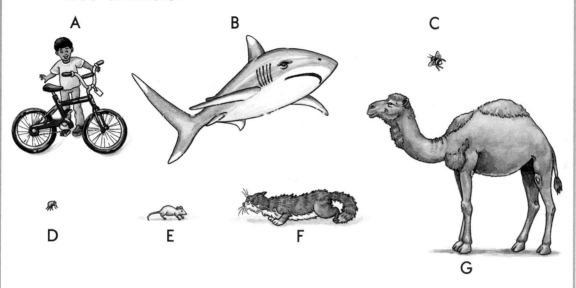

A
B
C
D
E
F
G

34

A

1
1. neither
2. remind
3. manage
4. prove

2
1. answered
2. learned
3. worried
4. managed

3
1. <u>be</u>come
2. <u>sobb</u>ing
3. <u>you</u>rself
4. <u>sound</u>ly
5. <u>dar</u>ling
6. <u>in</u>stead

4
1. couple
2. whirl
3. moments
4. important
5. expression
6. swirl

B

The Green Man Visits Nancy Again

Nancy was full. She didn't feel like climbing down from the counter top, so she just jumped. For Nancy, it was like jumping from the top of a building that is more than one hundred stories tall. But she landed on her feet as easily as you would if you jumped from a chair to the floor.

She walked back to her dollhouse. By the time she got back in bed, it was almost time for the sun to come up.

She wasn't very tired, but she made a decision to sleep. She closed her eyes, and in a few moments, she was sleeping soundly.

"Wake up, wake up," a loud voice said. Nancy opened her eyes. For a moment she didn't know where she was or what was standing in front of her. It was green and it was speaking in a loud voice, "Come on and wake up. Wake up."

"I'm awake," Nancy said. Her voice sounded thick and sleepy. The room was light. In fact, things looked so bright that Nancy had to cover her eyes. "Is that you?" she asked.

❀ The little green man answered, "Of course it's me. I've come to see if you're happy."

"No, I'm not happy," Nancy said.

"And why not?" the green man asked.

"Because I don't like being so little."

"Oh," the green man said and sat down. "I thought you never wanted to get big."

"I was wrong," Nancy replied. "I want to get big. I want to grow up. I want to be back with my parents and my friends."

The little green man said, "I can change you back to your regular size if I want to. But I'm not going to change you unless you tell me some things that you learned." The green man stood up and stared at Nancy. "What have you learned about kicking and screaming and acting like a baby?"

Nancy smiled. "I don't have to act like a baby because I can take care of myself."

The man said, "And when nobody is around, what do you do instead of kicking and crying?"

Nancy said, "You have to take care of yourself."

"Good," the green man said. "I'm glad that you learned things about yourself. But have you learned things about the world you live in?"

"Lots of things," Nancy said, and she began to list them. "I've learned that little things don't hurt themselves when they fall from high places. I've learned that . . . " Suddenly everything seemed to whirl and swirl around. Nancy tried to keep talking. "I've learned . . . " She felt very dizzy.

MORE NEXT TIME

C Number your paper from 1 through 20.

Skill Items

Write the word from the box that means the same thing as the underlined part of each sentence.

hoist	fish	tadpoles	squeak
remove	climb	moist	wrong

1. The pond is full of <u>baby frogs</u>.
2. The grass is <u>a little wet</u> today.
3. She will <u>take</u> the books from the desk.

Review Items

Some things happen as tadpoles grow.
4. Write the letter of what happens first.
5. Write the letter of what happens last.
   a. They grow front legs.
   b. Their tail disappears.
   c. They turn blue.
   d. They grow back legs.

6. The picture shows Goad filled up with air. Arrow A shows air leaving Goad this way ——→.
Write the letter of the arrow that shows the way Goad will move.

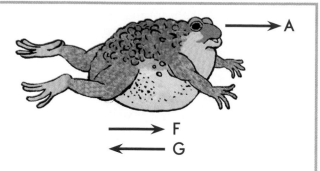

7. A mile is a little more than ▢ feet.

- 2 thousand
- 5 thousand
- 1 thousand

8. If an ant weighed as much as a cat, the ant could carry an object as heavy as ▢.

These animals fell from a cliff. Write the words that tell what happened to each animal.

- not hurt
- hurt
- killed

flea

9.　　10.　11.　　12.　　13.

14. Does a housefly weigh **more than a gram** or **less than a gram?**

15. Does a dog weigh **more than a gram** or **less than a gram?**

16. How many grams are on the left side of the scale?

17. So how much weight is on the side of the scale with the houseflies?

18. An arrow goes from the **F.** Which direction is that arrow going?

19. An arrow goes from the **G.** Which direction is that arrow going?

20. An arrow goes from the **J.** Which direction is that arrow going?

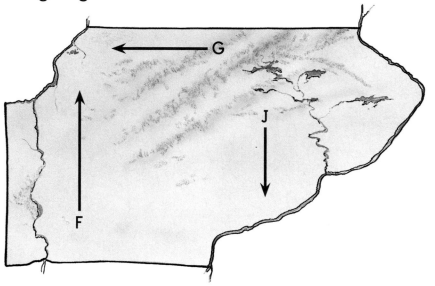

1	2	3
1. several	1. desk	1. expression
2. continue	2. snaps	2. darling
3. distance	3. prove	3. neither
4. sobbing	4. instead	4. becoming
5. worried	5. managed	5. important
6. couple	6. reminds	

B Sounds That Objects Make

In lesson 26 you read about Nancy's voice and what happened to it when she became smaller and smaller.

Here's the rule about your voice: **If you get smaller, your voice gets higher.**

Follow these instructions and you will see how sounds get higher when things get smaller.

1. Place a plastic ruler so that one end of it is on your desk and the other end hangs over the edge of the desk. Make sure that most of the ruler hangs over the desk. Picture 1 on the next page shows how to place the ruler on your desk.

2. Hold down the end of the ruler that is on the desk.

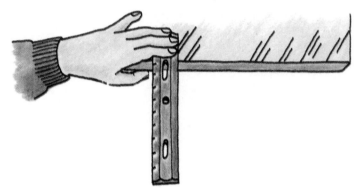

Picture 1

3. Bend the other end of the ruler down. Then let it go so it snaps back. The ruler will make a sound.

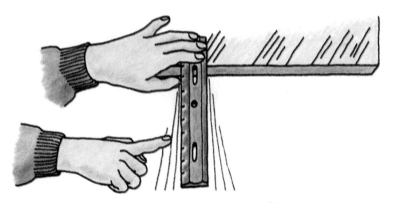

Picture 2

4. Now move the ruler so a smaller part of the ruler hangs over the edge of the desk. The ruler will make a sound that is higher.

5. Now move the ruler so that even less of the ruler hangs over the edge of the desk. The ruler will make a sound that is even higher.

The ruler works just like your voice. When your body gets smaller, the sound of your voice gets higher.

C Nancy Becomes Regular Size

The whole room seemed to be turning and swirling. Nancy felt so dizzy that she was afraid she would fall over. She kept trying to tell the little green man about the things she had learned. Finally, she managed to say, "I learned that water has a skin."

Nancy closed her eyes and talked very loudly. She hoped that she could stop the dizzy feeling by talking loudly.

Suddenly, Nancy opened her eyes. But she didn't see the little green man. She saw the face of a woman.

The expression on that woman's face was one of shock. Her eyes were wide open and so was her mouth. "Where . . . ," the woman said, "where have you been?"

The expression changed. Tears began to form in the woman's eyes. Then Nancy's mother threw her arms around Nancy. "Oh, Nancy," she said. Her voice was sobbing, and she was holding Nancy very tightly. "Oh, darling," she said. "We've been so worried . . ."

Nancy started to cry. She didn't want to cry, but she was so glad to see her mother, and it felt so good to have her mother hold her. She couldn't hold back the tears. "Oh, Mother," she said.

For a few minutes, neither Nancy nor ⭐ her mother said anything. Then, her mother grabbed Nancy's hands and held them tightly as she said, "Nancy, where have you been? The police have been looking for you and . . . And Sally told a crazy story about you becoming very small."

"It's true," Nancy said. "I know it sounds crazy, but I can prove to you that it really happened. I can tell you where the crumbs of toast are on the counter. I can tell you about the drops of water in the bathroom," Nancy said. "And I can tell you other things."

Nancy's mother was smiling and crying and laughing at the same time. "Oh, Nancy, I don't know what to believe, but I'm very glad to have my darling little baby back."

Nancy said, "I'm not a baby. That's the most important thing I learned when I was less than one centimeter tall. I can take care of myself. And I don't mind growing up at all."

That story took place a couple of years ago. Nancy is still growing up. And she's doing a fine job. She doesn't act like a baby—not even when things go wrong. Instead, she reminds herself, "I can take care of myself." And that's just what she does.

THE END

Skill Items

He is supposed to make a decision in a couple of days.

1. What part means **should**?

2. What word means **two**?

3. What part means **make up his mind**?

---

4. Write one way that tells how both objects are the same.

5. Write 2 ways that tell how object A is different from object B.

Object A   Object B

Review Items

Some of the lines in the box are one inch long and some are one centimeter long.

6. Write the letter of every line that is one inch long.

7. Write the letter of every line that is one centimeter long.

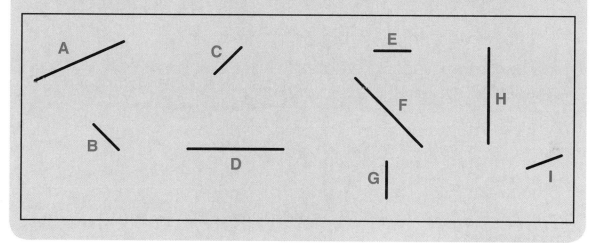

8. Which arrow shows the way the air will leave the jet engines?

9. Which arrow shows the way the jet will move?

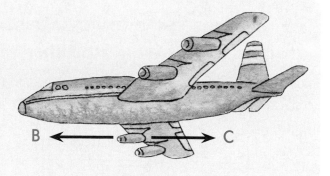

10. Write the letter of each water strider.

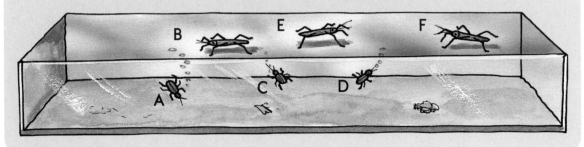

11. Is a water strider an insect?

12. How many legs does a water strider have?

13. How many legs does a fly have?

14. How many legs does a dog have?

15. How many legs does a spider have?

16. How many legs does an ant have?

17. When we weigh very small things, the unit we use is ▓▓▓▓.

Some things in the picture weigh **1 gram.** Some weigh **2 grams.** Some weigh **5 grams.** Write how much each object weighs.

18.　　　　　　19.　　　　　　20.

21.

22.

23. The food that 3 of the animals eat each day weighs more than those animals. Write the letters of those animals.

24. The food that 4 of the animals eat each day does not weigh as much as those animals. Write the letters of those animals.

A

1	2	3
1. a record	1. lifetime	1. fastest
2. cabbage	2. thrown	2. apart
3. maggot	3. tenth	3. worm
4. space	4. crawled	4. rotten
5. Herman	5. continued	5. several
		6. distance

B

Miles Per Hour

When we talk about **miles,** we tell how far apart things are. When we talk about **miles per hour,** we tell how fast things move.

The boat was three miles away. Does that tell how far or how fast?

The boat was going three miles per hour. Does that tell how far or how fast?

The faster something moves, the bigger the number of miles per hour. Ten is a bigger number than nine. So ten miles per hour is faster than nine miles per hour.

Look at pictures A, B, and C. The number below each dog shows how fast that dog is running.

How fast is dog A running?

How fast is dog B running?

How fast is dog C running?

Which dog is running fastest?

Which dog is in front of the others?

Is that dog the fastest dog?

A
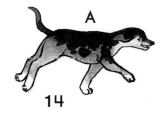
14

B
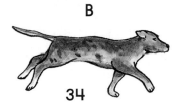
34

C
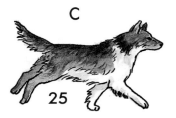
25

C A Push in the Opposite Direction

You've learned this rule: **The balloon moves in the opposite direction the air moves.**

You read about Goad. Here's the rule about Goad: **Goad moves in the opposite direction the air moves.** If the air comes out of Goad's mouth in this direction ———→, Goad moves in the opposite direction. She will move backwards, in this direction ←———.

If the air comes out of Goad's mouth in this direction ↙, in which direction will Goad move?

If the air coming out of Goad's mouth is blowing south, in which direction will Goad move?

If the air coming out of Goad's mouth is blowing down, in which direction will Goad move?

PICTURE 1   PICTURE 2

There is a rule like this one for everything that moves. Look at picture 1. The boy is standing on a block of ice. The boy is going to move in this direction: ⟶.

When ⭐ the boy starts to move in this direction ⟶, the block of ice will move in the opposite direction.

Look at picture 2. The arrow shows the boy moving in one direction and the ice moving in the opposite direction.

Look at picture 3. The girl wants to jump from the boat to the dock. Point to show which direction she will jump.

If she jumps in that direction, the boat will move in the opposite direction. When the boat moves in the opposite direction, the girl will fall in the water.

PICTURE 3

Picture 4 shows what happens when the girl tries to jump to the dock. In which direction did the girl start to move?

PICTURE 4

In which direction did the boat move?
Did the girl land on the dock?
The rule about how things move works for everything. **When something tries to move in one direction, something else tries to move in the opposite direction.**

D Number your paper from 1 through 25.

Each statement tells about **how far** something goes or **how fast** something goes. Write **how far** or **how fast** for each item.

1. They walked 6 miles.
2. They walked 6 miles per hour.
3. The bus was moving 20 miles per hour.
4. The bus was 20 miles from the city.

A 55   B 40   C 4   D 6

5. How fast is truck A going?
   • 55 hours   • 55 miles   • 55 miles per hour
6. How fast is truck B going?
   • 40 hours   • 40 miles   • 40 miles per hour
7. Which truck is going faster?
8. How fast is boy C going?
   • 4 hours   • 4 miles   • 4 miles per hour
9. How fast is boy D going?
   • 6 hours   • 6 miles   • 6 miles per hour
10. Which boy is going faster?

11. When we talk about miles per hour, we tell how ▒▒▒ something is moving.

Skill Items

Here are titles for different stories:
a. The Pink Flea   b. Pete Gets a Reward
c. The Ant That Escaped

12. One story tells about an insect that was a strange color. Write the letter of that title.

13. One story tells about an insect that got away from something. Write the letter of that title.

14. One story tells about someone who got something for doing a good job. Write the letter of that title.

Review Items

15. If you get smaller, your voice gets ▒▒▒.

16. Jean got smaller. So what do you know about Jean's voice?

17. Write the letter of the ruler that will make the lowest sound.

18. Write the letter of the ruler that will make the highest sound.

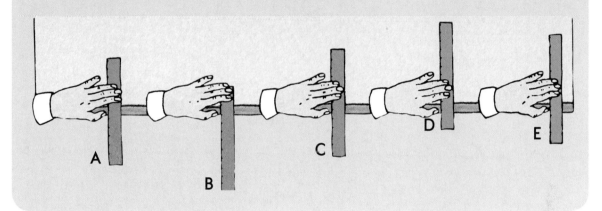

19. The food that a very small animal eats each day weighs ▢.
- less than the animal
- 5 pounds
- more than the animal

20. Does dew form in the middle of the day?

21. Dew forms when the air gets ▢.
- cooler
- windy
- warmer

22. What do all living things need?

23. What do all living things make?

24. Do all living things grow?

25. If tiny animals fall from high places, they don't ▢.

A

1
1. Kennedy Airport
2. speedometer
3. realized
4. busy
5. meant

2
1. crawled
2. changed
3. wiggled
4. buzzed
5. rubbed
6. rested

3
1. thrown
2. Herman's
3. tenth
4. sleepy
5. fly's

4
1. a record
2. per
3. laid
4. purse
5. lifetime

5
1. rotten
2. worm
3. maggot
4. space
5. crew
6. money

B More About Pushes in the Opposite Direction

You've learned that if something tries to move in one direction, something else tries to move in the opposite direction.

A paddle works that way. You move the paddle through the water. If the paddle moves through the water in this direction ⟶, the boat moves in the opposite direction. It moves in this direction ⟵.

A jet engine works the same way. The jet engine pushes air toward the back of the plane. The plane moves in the opposite direction. The faster the jet engines shoot air toward the back of the plane, the faster the plane moves forward.

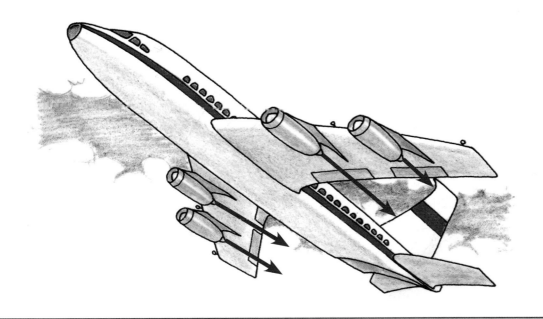

C Herman the Fly

Herman was a fly. He was born on some old cabbage leaves that had been thrown out. Herman's mother laid eggs on the leaves, and two days after she laid them, Herman was born. He had brothers and sisters. In fact, he had 80 brothers and 90 sisters. All Herman's brothers and sisters were born on those rotten cabbage leaves.

Right after Herman was born, he didn't look like he did when he was a full-grown fly. At first Herman looked like a worm because he was a worm. Here's the fact: When flies are born, they are worms called maggots.

For nine days, Herman was a maggot that crawled around on the cabbage eating and eating and eating. On the tenth day Herman felt sleepy. He stopped eating and went to sleep. When he woke up, he had changed. He was a fly. He wiggled out of his old maggot skin, and there he was, a fly. He was one centimeter long. Like all flies, he had six legs and two big eyes.

Here is something that you may not know about flies. Flies do not change size on the outside. But they change size on the inside. ✦ When Herman first became a fly, he was just as big as he was when he was an old, old fly. A fly's outside body is like a shell. Inside that shell is the part of the fly that grows. At first, the inside part is small. It looks like a little tiny foot in a great big shoe. There is lots of space between the part that grows and the shell. As the fly gets older and older, the inside part gets bigger and bigger until it fills up the shell.

A   B

Anyhow, it didn't take Herman long to grow up. Within nine days he was full-grown and doing those things that flies like to do. He buzzed around. He ate. He loved to find things that were rotten and warm. He rubbed his two front feet together as he rested.

Herman looked like any other fly. But he was different, very different. Herman has the record of flying farther and faster than any fly that has ever lived. Most flies fly a few hundred miles in their lifetime. A few flies will fly over a thousand miles. Herman flew thousands and thousands of miles. In the next story, you'll find out how he did that.

MORE NEXT TIME

D Number your paper from 1 through 21.

Review Items

1. A mile is more than ▆▆▆▆ feet.

   • 2 thousand   • 1 thousand   • 5 thousand

2. What part of the world is shown on the map?

3. The map shows how far apart some places are. One line shows 13 hundred miles. The other line shows 25 hundred miles. How far is it from **B** to **T**?

4. How far is it from **G** to **H**?

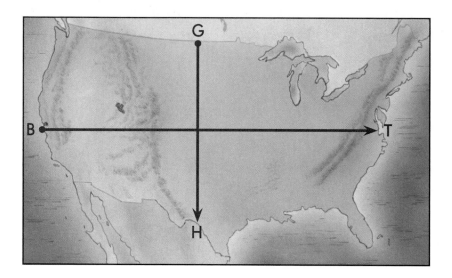

5. Which letter shows where the ground gets warm first?
6. Which letter shows where the ground gets warm last?

7. Which has a tall straight trunk, a forest tree or an apple tree?
8. Which has larger branches, a forest tree or an apple tree?
9. Which is longer, a centimeter or an inch?

10. Write the letter of each toad in the picture.

11. Write the letter of each frog in the picture.

12. Write the letter of each mole in the picture.

13. Which animal has smooth skin, a frog or a toad?

14. Which animal can jump farther, a frog or a toad?

15. Do any frogs have teeth?

16. If an ant weighed as much as a desk, the ant could carry an object as heavy as ░░░░.

17. You can see drops of water on grass early in the morning. What are those drops called?

18. Which weighs more, one gram or one water strider?

19. About how many ants would it take to weigh one gram?

20. Roots keep a tree from ░░░░.

21. Roots carry ░░░░ to all parts of the tree.

A

1
1. San Francisco
2. passenger
3. attendant
4. pilot
5. idea

2
1. flew
2. chew
3. blew
4. crew

3
1. <u>under</u>stand
2. <u>taxi</u>cab
3. <u>sun</u>light
4. <u>air</u>plane
5. <u>be</u>long

4
1. traffic
2. realized
3. busy
4. speedometer
5. hung

5
1. Kennedy Airport
2. money
3. driver
4. meant
5. purse

6
1. S-shaped
2. bounce
3. bouncing
4. jumbo
5. travel

Speedometers

You know that miles per hour tells how fast something is moving. The faster something is moving, the bigger the numbers.

Which is moving faster, something that goes five miles per hour or something that goes four miles per hour?

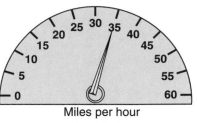

PICTURE 1

Picture 1 shows a speedometer inside a car that is moving. The arrow is pointing to a number. That number tells how fast the car is going.

Picture 2 shows a speedometer inside a car that is not moving. That car is going zero miles per hour.

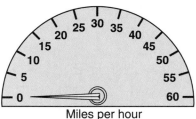

PICTURE 2

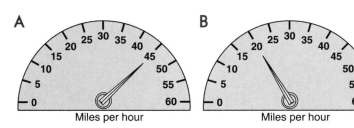

PICTURE 3

C

Herman Goes to Kennedy Airport

Herman became the fly that flew farther than any other fly. If you want to understand how this happened, you have to know where Herman lived.

Herman was born in New York City. He was born on a cabbage leaf that was about five miles from a large airport called Kennedy Airport. Kennedy Airport is very busy. You can go to Kennedy Airport at any time of the day or night and see planes. Some are in the sky, getting ready to land. Others are on the ground, getting ready to take off.

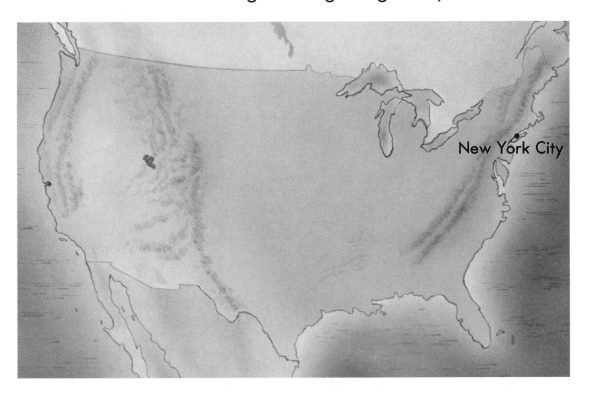

New York City

Herman went to Kennedy Airport. Five miles is pretty far for a fly to travel, but Herman didn't fly all the way. He was buzzing around, looking for food, when he saw a nice, warm yellow. He didn't know what it was, but it was warm and yellow. So he landed on it.

It was a shiny new taxicab that was on its way to the airport. It was stopped at a traffic light when Herman landed on the roof. When the cab began to move, Herman thought he would fly away, but then he realized that the wind was blowing too fast. Here's the rule: The faster the cab moves, the faster the wind blows on Herman. ⭐

Flies don't take off when the wind is blowing very fast. Flies use their six legs to hang on as hard as they can. So Herman hung on as hard as he could, and the wind blew and blew. But soon the wind blew slower and slower. And then the wind stopped.

The cab had stopped at the airport. For Herman, this stop meant that he could fly away from the cab. For the two women inside the cab, this stop meant that they would have to start working. The women were part of the crew of a jumbo jet.

One of the women opened her purse. She took out some money to pay the cab driver. The sun was shining on the things in her opened purse. There was a pack of chewing gum. And there was some candy. CANDY. If there is one thing that flies love more than cabbage leaves and rotten meat, it is candy. And in the warm sunlight, what could be better than a piece of candy that is four times bigger than you are? Herman saw that piece of candy. He made two circles in the air and one S-shaped move. And he landed right on the candy. But just as he was ready to start eating, everything got dark.

MORE NEXT TIME

D Number your paper from 1 through 18.

Skill Items

Here's the rule: **Toads have warts.**

1. Zorm is a toad. So what does the rule tell you about Zorm?

2. Gleeb is not a toad. So what does the rule tell you about Gleeb?

Write the word from the box that means the same thing as the underlined part of each sentence.

apart	warts	behind	motioned	
ahead	propped	hair	broiled	boasted

3. She <u>bragged</u> about winning the race.
4. The cab was <u>in front</u> of the bus.
5. The animal was covered with <u>little bumps</u>.

Things that are this far apart on the map ←——→ are 1 mile apart.

Things that are this far apart ←————————→ are 2 miles apart.

6. How far is it from the pool to the park?

7. How far is it from the park to the forest?

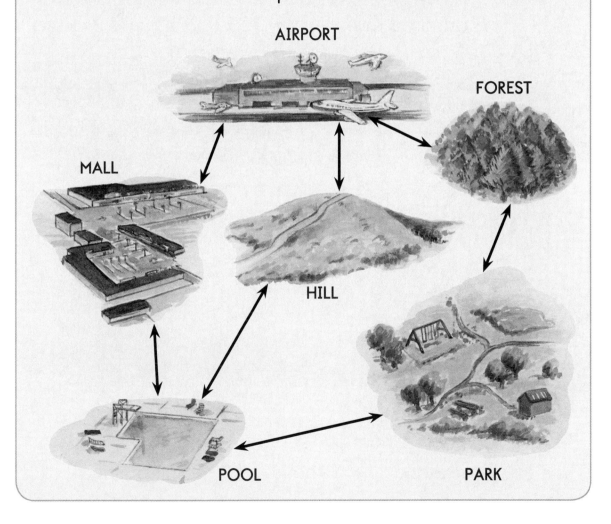

8. What part of the world is shown on the map?

9. The map shows how far apart some places are. How far is it from **M** to **P?**
   - 13 hundred miles
   - 35 hundred miles
   - 25 hundred miles

10. How far is it from **X** to **Y?**
    - 13 hundred miles
    - 35 hundred miles
    - 25 hundred miles

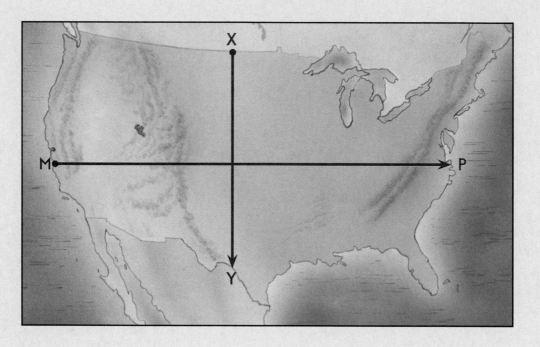

11. A mile is more than ▢ feet.
    - 5 thousand
    - 3 thousand
    - 1 thousand

Each statement tells about how far something goes or how fast something goes. Write **how far** or **how fast** for each item.

12. She walked 3 miles.

13. The bus was going 50 miles per hour.

14. She walked 3 miles per hour.

15. He chased the dog 6 miles.

16. How **fast** is truck **R** going?

17. How **fast** is truck **S** going?

18. Which truck is going faster?

R

S

25

30

A

1
1. insect
2. engine
3. fastened
4. peaceful
5. thermometer

2
1. passengers
2. brewed
3. tossed
4. rules
5. cities
6. bouncing

3
1. a record
2. San Francisco
3. per
4. attendant
5. pilot
6. boiling

4
1. flight
2. idea
3. crack
4. member
5. chewing
6. thaw

B Airplane Crew Members

Here's a picture of some airplane crew members.

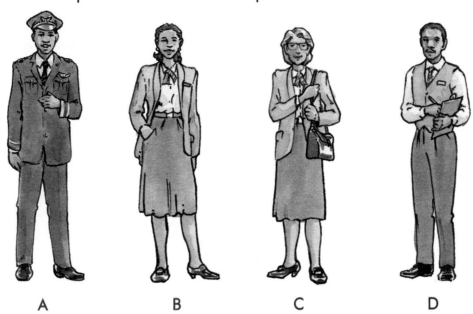

A   B   C   D

A is the pilot. The others are flight attendants.

On a large jumbo jet, there may be fifteen flight attendants.

Here are some facts:

- The pilot and some other crew members work in the front of the plane. They fly the plane.
- The flight attendants work in the back of the plane. They take care of the passengers.

Herman Ends Up on a Jumbo Jet

For the next part of Herman's story, you have to know something about the United States. Kennedy Airport is in New York City. And New York City is on the east side of the United States.

There are cities on the west side of the United States. One of them is San Francisco.

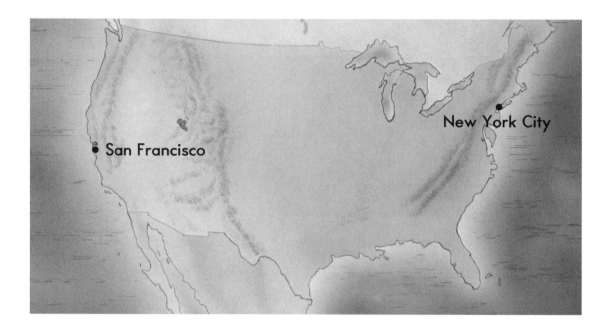

Herman was in a purse. That purse belonged to a member of a jumbo jet crew. The woman had closed the purse, and Herman couldn't get out.

At first, Herman didn't like the idea of being inside a dark place, but then he thought he would try to have a good time anyhow. So he started to eat the candy. Eating it was a little hard because things kept bouncing up and down and up and down. The crew members were walking through the airport on their way to their jumbo jet.

That jumbo jet was going to fly from New York City all the way to San Francisco. Touch the map on page 246. Show where the jet starts out and where it will land. ⭐

The trip from New York City to San Francisco is about 25 hundred miles.

Herman kept trying to eat as the purse bounced up and down. Then suddenly everything went this way and that way. The crew member had tossed her purse on a shelf inside the jumbo jet. Herman didn't like to be tossed around like that. "Let me out of this dark," he thought to himself and tried to fly out of the purse.

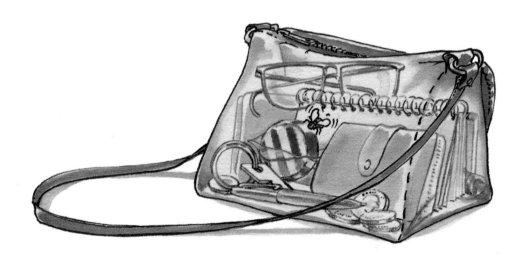

🌸 He bounced around for a while, and then his eyes saw a crack where light was coming in. Herman ran up the inside of the purse and went through the crack. There were smells in the air, but most of them did not smell very good to Herman. They were the clean smells of clean seats and clean floors and clean windows.

Herman took off to find some better smells or some better light. He found a nice, warm red. It was fuzzy and very warm. Herman took a nap. He was on the back of a seat, right next ✿ to the window. The sun was shining through the window. That felt great.

MORE NEXT TIME

D Number your paper from 1 through 22.

Skill Items

> **Several paths continued for a great distance.**
> 1. What part means a **long way?**
> 2. What word refers to more than two but less than a lot?
> 3. What word means **kept on going?**

Review Items

4. What color are the flowers that apple trees make?
5. What grows in each place where there was a flower?

6. Which has a tall straight trunk, a forest tree or an apple tree?

7. How many years could it take for a forest to grow back after a forest fire?

- 10 years
- 200 years
- 100 years

Some things happen as tadpoles grow.
8. Write the letter of what happens first.
9. Write the letter of what happens last.

   a. Their tail disappears.
   b. They grow front legs.
   c. They grow back legs.

10. Write the letter of each statement that is make-believe.

    a. A toad flew away.
    b. A bird flew away.
    c. A dog flew away.
    d. A fly flew away.

11. When we talk about miles per hour, we tell how ▮▮▮ something is moving.

12. A speedometer tells about ▮▮▮.

- hours
- miles per hour
- miles

Some of the lines in the box are one inch long and some are one centimeter long.

13. Write the letter of every line that is one centimeter long.

14. Write the letter of every line that is one inch long.

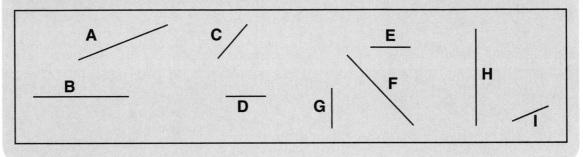

15. Which is longer, a centimeter or a meter?

16. How many centimeters long is a meter?

17. Write the letters of the 4 names that tell about length.

a. inch   d. day   g. hour   i. mile
b. year   e. second   h. week   j. minute
c. centimeter   f. meter

18. What part of the world is shown on the map?

The map shows how far apart some places are. One line shows 13 hundred miles. The other line shows 25 hundred miles.

19. How far is it from **A** to **B**?

20. How far is it from **C** to **D**?

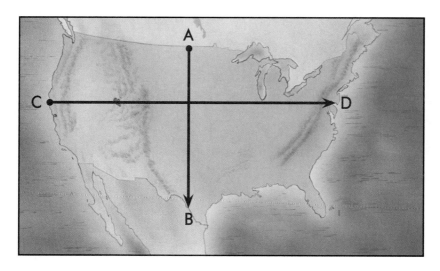

21. Arrow **X** shows the direction the boy will jump. Which arrow shows the direction the block of ice will move?

22. Arrow B shows the direction the girl will jump. Which arrow shows the direction the boat will move?

Number your paper from 1 through 26.

Some hairs in the picture are being pushed down. Some are being pulled up. Look at the skin around each hair.
  1. Write the letter of each hair that is being pushed down.
  2. Write the letter of each hair that is being pulled up.

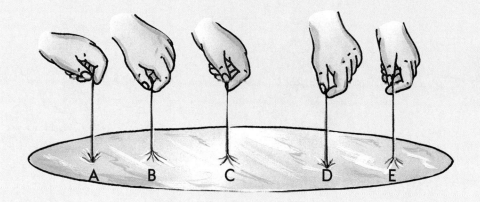

  3. When we weigh very small things, the unit we use is ▮▮▮▮.

4. The food that 3 of the animals eat each day weighs more than those animals. Write the letters of those animals.

5. The food that 4 of the animals eat each day does not weigh as much as those animals. Write the letters of those animals.

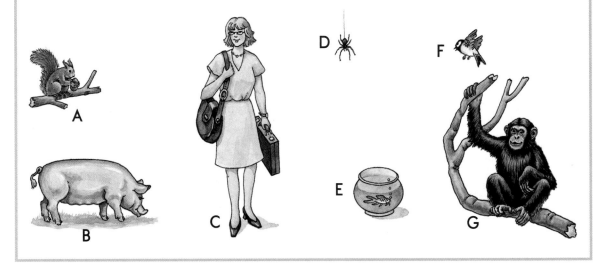

6. If you get smaller, your voice gets ▮▮▮.

7. Tom got smaller. So what do you know about Tom's voice?

8. Write the letter of the ruler that will make the highest sound.

9. Write the letter of the ruler that will make the lowest sound.

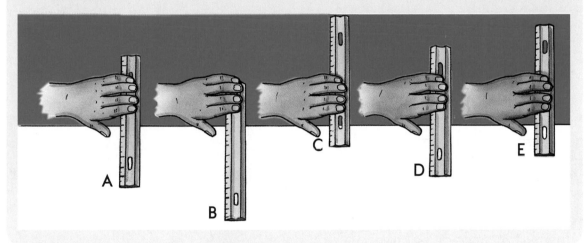

Each statement tells about how far something goes or how fast something goes. Write **how far** or **how fast** for each item.

10. He ran 5 miles per hour.

11. He ran 5 miles.

12. The plane was 500 miles from New York City.

13. The plane was flying 500 miles per hour.

14. When we talk about miles per hour, we tell how ▆▆▆▆ something is moving.

15. When something tries to move in one direction, something else tries to move ▆▆▆▆.

16. How fast is car **A** going?

17. How fast is car **B** going?

18. Which car is going faster?

A   B

25   30

19. How far is it from New York City to San Francisco?

Skill Items

Look at object A and object B.

20. Write one way that tells how both objects are the same.

21. Write 2 ways that tell how object A is different from object B.

Object A   Object B

For each item, write the underlined word or words from the sentences in the box.

> The <u>traffic</u> was moving forty miles <u>per</u> hour. He is <u>supposed to</u> <u>make a decision</u> in a <u>couple</u> of days.

22. What underlining means **two?**
23. What underlining means **each?**
24. What underlining means **make up his mind?**
25. What underlining refers to all the cars and trucks that were moving on the street?
26. What underlining means **should?**

END OF TEST 4

41

A

1
1. Lake Michigan
2. Chicago
3. temperature
4. building
5. super
6. frightened

2
1. supposed
2. insects
3. fastened
4. livings
5. peaceful

3
1. brushed
2. engines
3. seated
4. belts
5. boiling

4
1. <u>take</u>off
2. <u>butter</u>fly
3. <u>grass</u>hopper
4. <u>W</u>-shaped

5
1. couple
2. beetle
3. spider
4. speed
5. thermometer

6
1. begun
2. flown
3. thaw
4. ice

B

Insects

Most bugs are insects. Some bugs are not insects.

An ant is an insect. A fly is an insect. A butterfly is an insect. A beetle, a bee, and a grasshopper are insects. Spiders are not insects.

Here are the rules about all insects:
- An insect has six legs.
- The body of an insect has three parts.

An ant has six legs. Its body has three parts. So an ant is an insect.

A fly has six legs. Its body has three parts. So a fly is an insect.

A spider has eight legs. Its body has two parts. So a spider is not an insect.

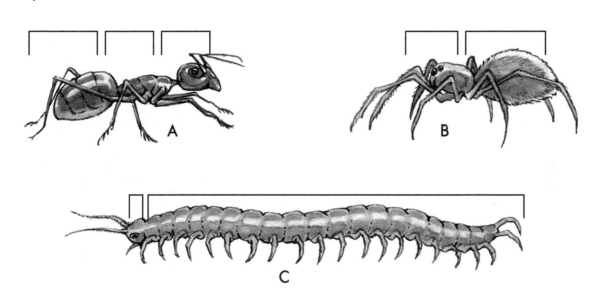

A

B

C

C **Facts About** Speed

When you tell how fast something is moving, you tell about the speed of that thing. Here are facts about speed:
- A fast man can run 20 miles per hour.
- A fast dog can run 35 miles per hour.
- A racing car can go 200 miles per hour.
- A jumbo jet flies 500 miles per hour.

D Getting Ready for Takeoff

Herman was on a plane that was on the east side of the United States. That plane was going to a city on the west side of the United States.

Herman was taking a nap on a warm red. Suddenly something told him that he was in danger. A big dark was dropping on him. "You're not going to get me," Herman thought and took off just as the big dark dropped next to him.

Then he ran into a living. That was bad. Herman liked to land on livings, but he didn't like to run into them. Then there was more danger. The living came after him. Herman did a W-shaped move and he got away from the living.

Here's what had happened. The passengers had begun to get on the plane. One of them dropped a coat on the seat back where Herman was. If Herman hadn't flown away, the coat would have landed on him.

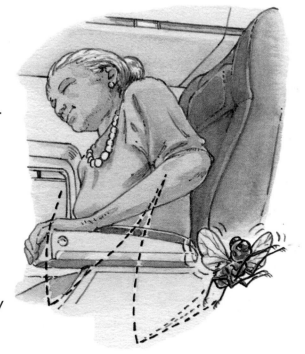

Then as Herman was trying to get away ✦ from the coat, he flew right into the face of another passenger. That passenger tried to brush Herman away with her hand.

Now Herman was flying around, trying to find a peaceful place in the sun, but he couldn't seem to find one. In every place he went there were lots of livings. He tried to land on a couple of livings, but they brushed him away. He didn't know it, but there were three hundred people on this jumbo jet, and the plane was getting ready to take off.

The flight attendants were making sure that all the passengers were seated and they were wearing their seat belts. One flight attendant was telling passengers what they were supposed to do if the plane was in danger.

Now the great jet engines of the plane were starting up. Outside, the sound was so loud that you would have to hold your hands over your ears. But to the passengers inside the plane the sound of the engines was no louder than a noisy car engine.

MORE NEXT TIME

E Number your paper from 1 through 18.

Skill Items

Here's a rule: **Fish live in water.**
1. Alex is not a fish. So what does the rule tell you about Alex?
2. A trout is a fish. So what does the rule tell you about a trout?
3. A lizard is not a fish. So what does the rule tell you about a lizard?

Use the words in the box to write complete sentences.

continued	cleared	supposed	service	distance
decision	dead	couple	quite	several

4. He is ▮▮▮ to make a ▮▮▮ in a ▮▮▮ of days.
5. ▮▮▮ paths ▮▮▮ for a great ▮▮▮.

Review Items
6. A mile is more than ▮▮▮ feet.
   - 1 thousand   • 5 thousand   • 2 thousand
7. What part of a car tells how fast the car is moving?

Here's how fast different things can go:
- 20 miles per hour
- 35 miles per hour
- 200 miles per hour
- 500 miles per hour

8. Which speed tells how fast a jet can fly?

9. Which speed tells how fast a fast dog can run?

10. Which speed tells how fast a fast man can run?

11. What part of the world is shown on the map?

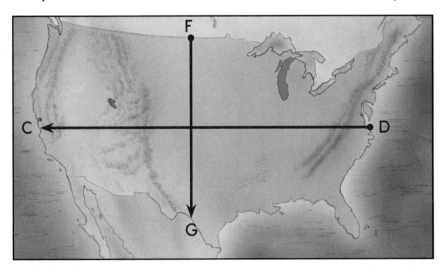

12. The map shows how far apart some places are. How far is it from **F** to **G?**

The speedometers are in two different cars.

A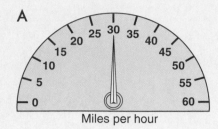

B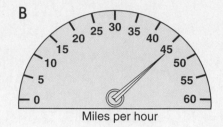

13. How fast is car A going?

14. How fast is car B going?

15. Which car is going faster?

16. Which weighs more, one gram or one water strider?

17. How many ants would it take to weigh one gram?

18. Arrow B shows the direction the girl will jump. Which arrow shows the direction the boat will move?

1

1. degrees
2. service
3. captain
4. weather
5. oven

2

1. buildings
2. boiling
3. hearts
4. pounding
5. trays

3

1. <u>for</u>ward
2. <u>run</u>way
3. <u>down</u>town
4. <u>them</u>selves
5. <u>next</u>-hottest
6. <u>loud</u>speaker

4

1. Denver
2. temperature
3. wing
4. frightened
5. super
6. salad

Temperature

When we talk about how hot or cold something is, we tell about the temperature of the thing.

Something that is very hot has a high temperature. Something that is very cold has a low temperature.

Is the temperature of ice high or low?

Is the temperature of boiling water high or low?

Here's the rule: **When an object gets hotter, the temperature goes up.**

Object A gets hotter. So what do you know about the temperature of object A?

When a floor gets cold, which way does the temperature go?

A glass of water gets hotter. Tell about the temperature.

C Herman Takes Off
for San Francisco

The jet engines on a jumbo jet work the same way that Goad works when she wants to move very fast. When Goad got away from the Brown family, she let the air rush out. The air rushed out one way, and Goad went flying the other way. That's just how jet engines work. The air rushes out of the back of the engine. The engine moves in the opposite direction—**forward.** The engine is on the wing, so the wing moves forward. The wing is on the plane, so the plane moves forward.

When jet engines work, they make a great, loud sound. The plane goes down the runway, faster and faster. The people inside try to act as if they are not frightened, but their hearts start pounding faster. The people begin to wonder how a plane that is almost as big as a school can take off and fly like a bird. Racing cars go two hundred

miles per hour. The jet plane goes faster than most racing cars while the plane is still on the runway.

Then the passengers look out the windows and have trouble believing what they see.  They see their city, but it looks like a toy city—with tiny cars and buildings that look so small you could pick them up. The plane circles around, and the passengers look at the buildings in downtown New York. "Wow," they say to themselves.

Then the plane goes up and up until it is six miles above the ground. Think of it. Six miles high.

Now, a flight attendant talks to the passengers.

"You may remove your seat belts and move around the plane now." The passengers start to talk to each other now. They feel safe. The plane doesn't seem to be moving at all. Walking around inside the plane is just like walking around inside a building. But the passengers inside the plane are moving along at the speed of five hundred miles per hour.

Herman was moving at five hundred miles per hour. But he wasn't thinking much about it. He didn't feel like a super fly. In fact, he wasn't the only fly in that jumbo jet. Like most jumbo jets that fly in the summer, it had flies in it. There were six flies and one beetle.

MORE NEXT TIME

D Number your paper from 1 through 27.

Story Items

1. Pretend you are in an airplane that is flying over a city. What would look different about the city?
   - Things would be darker.
   - Things would be smaller.
   - Things would be bigger.

Skill Items

Here are the titles of some stories:
       a. Glenn Found Gold
       b. Four Skunks Under the House
       c. The Day Uncle Bill Came to Visit

2. One story tells about a bad, bad smell. Write the letter of that title.

3. One story tells about a man who went to somebody's home. Write the letter of that title.

4. One story tells about a man who became very rich. Write the letter of that title.

Write the word from the box that means the same thing as the underlined part of each sentence.

spider	apart	couple	per	weather
pilot	insect	passenger	service	

5. Tom picked fifty apples <u>each</u> hour.
6. The <u>bug with six legs</u> walked up my arm.
7. The <u>person who flew the plane</u> told about the trip.

Review Items

Here's how fast different things can go:
- 20 miles per hour
- 35 miles per hour
- 200 miles per hour
- 500 miles per hour

8. Which speed tells how fast a racing car can go?

9. Which speed tells how fast a jet can fly?

10. Which speed tells how fast a fast man can run?

11. Which animal has smooth skin, a frog or a toad?

12. Which animal can jump farther, a toad or a frog?

13. A speedometer tells about ▧▧▧.
- hours   • miles   • miles per hour

14. Write the names of the 4 insects.
- spider   • bird   • beetle   • bee   • snake
- toad   • fly   • worm   • ant

15. How many parts does the body of an insect have?

16. How many legs does an insect have?

17. How many legs does a spider have?

18. How many parts does a spider's body have?

19. What's the boiling temperature of water?
- 112 degrees   • 121 miles   • 212 degrees

20. When something tries to move in one direction, something else tries to move ▧▧▧.

21. Arrow **X** shows the direction the boy will jump. Which arrow shows the direction the block of ice will move?

22. When we weigh very small things, the unit we use is ▮▮▮▮.

Some things in the picture weigh **1 gram.** Some weigh **2 grams.** Some weigh **5 grams.** Write how much each object weighs.

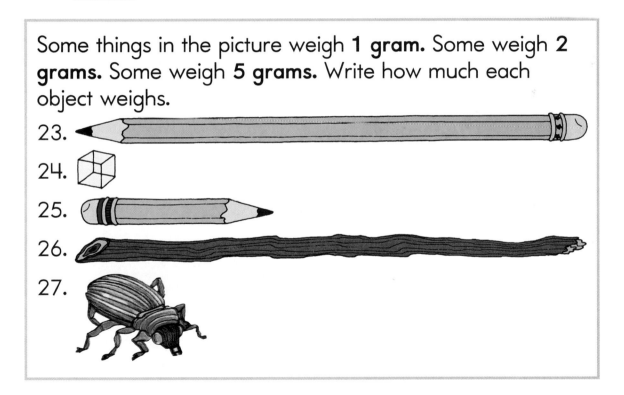

23.

24.

25.

26.

27.

A

1
1. coldest
2. degrees
3. cooking
4. trays
5. passed
6. kills

2
1. coast
2. galley
3. Denver
4. service
5. perfect
6. panel

3
1. Lake Michigan
2. captain
3. Chicago
4. salad
5. coffee

4
1. oven
2. spray
3. stuff
4. shrimp
5. metal

5
1. figure
2. quite
3. stack
4. return

B

Degrees

When an object gets hotter, does the temperature of the object go up or down?

We measure temperature in degrees. Here's the rule: When the temperature goes up, the number of degrees gets bigger.

Look at the picture. It tells how many degrees each object is.

A
40 degrees

B
10 degrees

C
70 degrees

The hottest object has the biggest number of degrees.

On a hot summer day, the temperature may reach 100 degrees. On a cold winter day when cars won't start, the temperature may get down to zero degrees.

The temperature inside your school is about 70 degrees.

C

Herman Lands in San Francisco

Sometimes flies get inside jumbo jets. And sometimes these flies will go all the way across the United States. That's what happened to Herman. He went from a city on the east coast to a city on the west coast. And he wasn't the only fly on that trip.

When the plane was over Chicago, the captain talked over the loudspeaker to the passengers. "Look below and you can see the city of Chicago. That lake you see next to Chicago is Lake Michigan."

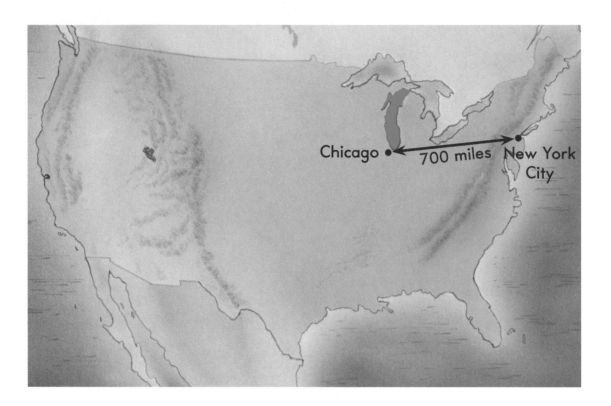

Herman wasn't looking at any lakes. He was trying to find something to eat. He could smell some really good stuff.

The crew was brewing coffee and cooking dinner for the passengers. It didn't take Herman very long to find the place where the food was. On a plane, that place is not called a kitchen. It is called a galley. The galley was warm, and it smelled great to Herman.

"We're going to begin our meal service now," a crew member said. "So please return to your seats."

Herman had already started his meal service. He started with a salad that had some shrimp in it. "Good," he thought to himself. Then he went to a piece of cheese. "Good, good," he thought to himself. ⭐ Did that fly ever eat!

When the meal service was over, it was time for a nap. Herman found the perfect place. It was a metal panel next to the oven. It was very warm—just right.

Herman napped for the rest of the trip. The crew members put away the food trays. They cleaned up the galley, and Herman had to get out of their way a couple of times. But he flew back to his nice warm metal panel and had a good rest. The trip from New York City to San Francisco took six hours. After the plane passed over Chicago, it went west over Denver, and then over Salt Lake City. And then it landed in San Francisco.

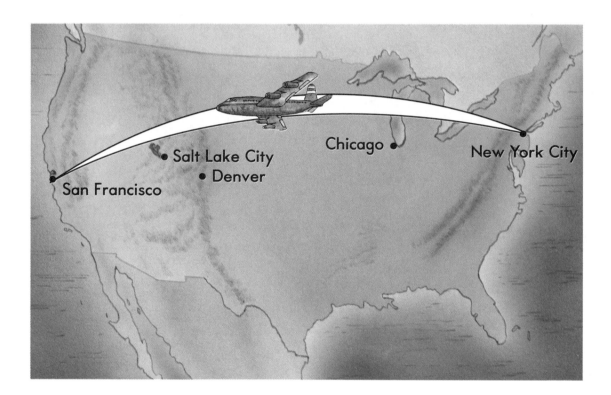

When the plane landed in San Francisco, the passengers got off and said thank you to the crew members. Then the crew members got off and said, "Am I glad to be home." Then three flies got off.

After the crew left the plane four men and three women came into the plane and cleaned up. They also filled the air with a spray that kills flies.

MORE NEXT TIME

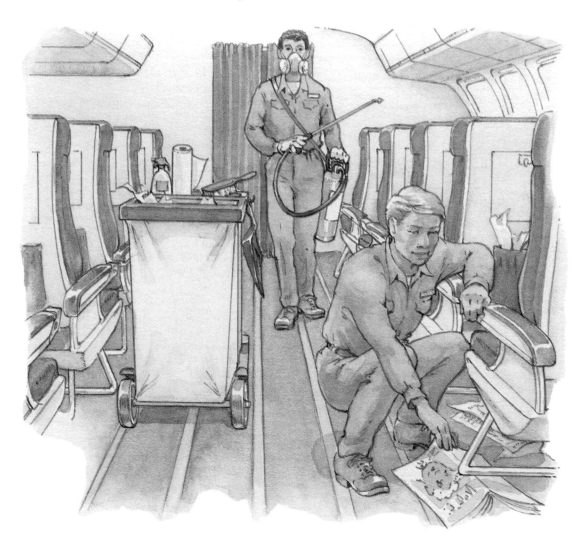

Number your paper from 1 through 24.

Story Items

Look at the picture. It tells how many degrees each object is.
  1. Which object is the hottest?
  2. What is the temperature of that object?
  3. Which object is coldest?
  4. What is the temperature of that object?

A    B    C

20 degrees   60 degrees   35 degrees

  5. When an object gets hotter, the temperature goes ▮▮▮▮.

  6. When the temperature goes up, what gets bigger?
    • the number of degrees
    • the number of miles per hour
    • the time

Skill Items

Here's a rule: **Every insect has six legs.**

7. Jub is an insect. So what does the rule tell you about Jub?

8. Frig is not an insect. So what does the rule tell you about Frig?

Boiling water will thaw ice in a few moments.

9. What word means **melt**?

10. What 2 words mean **not very many seconds**?

11. What word tells you that the water was 212 degrees?

Review Items

Each statement tells about how far something goes or how fast something goes. Write **how far** or **how fast** for each item.

12. The car that won the race drove 200 miles per hour.

13. The woman ran 3 miles to get home.

14. The dog was running 35 miles per hour.

15. They drove 200 miles without stopping.

16. Write the names of the 4 insects.

- fish
- beetle
- fly
- spider
- bird
- frog
- bee
- snake
- worm
- ant

17. How many legs does an insect have?
18. How many parts does the body of an insect have?
19. How many parts does a spider's body have?
20. How many legs does a spider have?
21. When we talk about how hot or cold something is, we tell about the ____ of the thing.

- length
- weight
- temperature

22. When an object gets hotter, the temperature goes ____.

23. The arrow on the thermometer shows that the temperature is going down. Is the water getting **hotter** or **colder?**

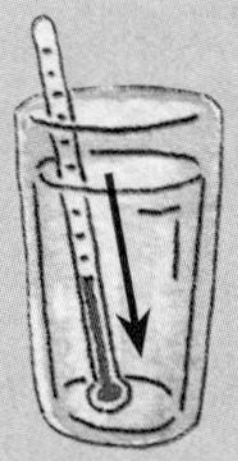

24. The arrow on the thermometer shows that the temperature is going up. Is the water getting **hotter** or **colder?**

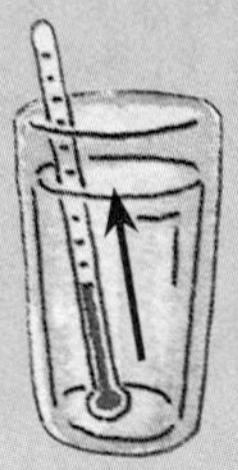

1
1. although
2. copilot
3. ocean
4. figure
5. gentlemen

2
1. finding
2. cleared
3. facing
4. workers
5. stacked

3
1. weren't
2. decision
3. weather
4. galley
5. coast

4
1. perfect
2. panel
3. dead
4. quite
5. frozen

5
1. dodge
2. flown
3. huge
4. June

B Finding the Direction of a Wind

To find the direction of a wind, you face the wind so the wind blows in your face.

The direction you're facing tells the name of the wind. If you face east, the wind is an **east wind.** If you face north, the wind is a **north wind.**

Look at picture A. The arrows show the direction the wind is blowing. The cow is facing into the wind.

Which direction is the cow facing?

So what's the name of the wind?

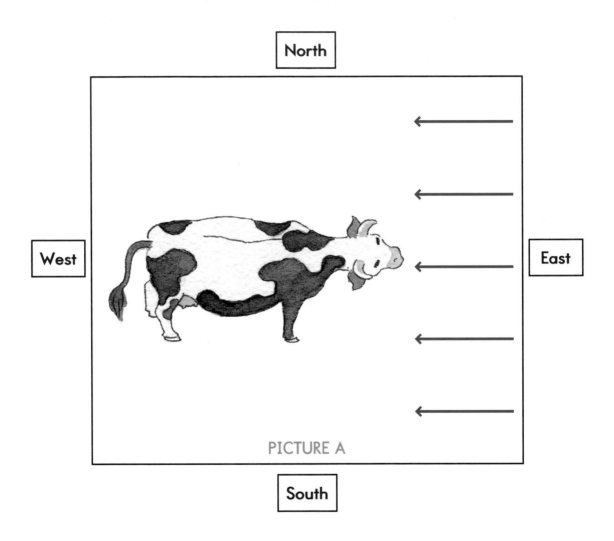

North

West

East

PICTURE A

South

Look at picture B. The arrows show the wind. Which animal is facing into the wind?

Which direction is that animal facing?

So what's the name of the wind?

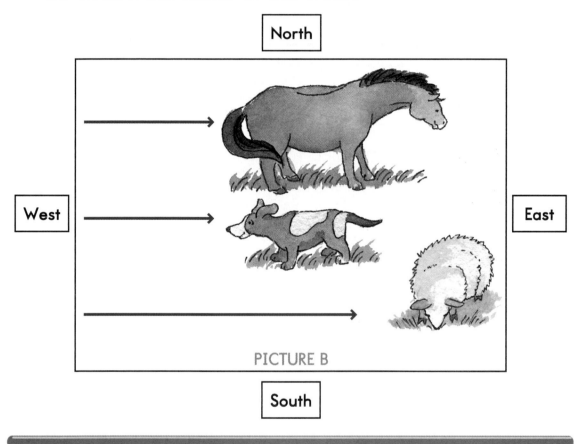

North

West

East

PICTURE B

South

C Fly Spray Fills the Air

Herman and five other flies were on the jumbo jet when it landed in San Francisco. Some of the flies got off the plane in San Francisco. Shortly after the plane pulled up to the gate, some men and women came into the plane and cleaned it. They filled the air with fly spray. When the air cleared and the workers left the plane, there were two dead flies. One fly felt quite well. This fly had been sitting on a warm metal panel in the galley. That panel was close to an outside door. Two workers had opened that door and then started to load the dinners for the next flight. Fresh air blew in through the open door. This air kept the fly spray from reaching Herman. Herman didn't know that the air saved his life.

The workers stacked the dinners next to Herman. The dinners didn't smell very good because they were frozen, and flies do not like things that are too cold. The air was too cold for Herman. While it was blowing on him, he kept thinking, "This air is too cold. I should fly to a warmer place." Every time he got ready to take off, the air stopped blowing so hard and he could feel the nice warm panel. So he made a decision to stay on the metal panel.

If Herman had felt a nice warm breeze and sunlight outside, he would have flown out the open door. But on that day, the weather in San Francisco was as cool as it usually is. Here's why the weather is usually cool in San Francisco. San Francisco is next to the ocean. The air over the ocean is cool. The air blows from the ocean to San Francisco. So, San Francisco is cool.

The jet that Herman was on was going back to New York City. That jet would go faster on the trip to New York City. Here's why. The jet was going to fly in the same direction the wind was blowing.

MORE NEXT TIME

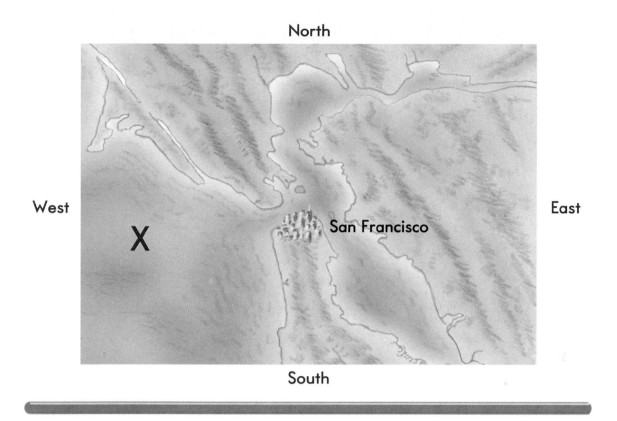

North

West

X

San Francisco

East

South

D Number your paper from 1 through 25.

Story Items

1. How many hours did it take to fly from New York City to San Francisco?
2. Will it take **more time** or **less time** to fly from San Francisco to New York City?

3. Would a plane fly **faster** or **slower** when it goes in the same direction as the wind?

4. When the plane flies from San Francisco to New York City, is it flying in the **same direction** or the **opposite direction** as the wind?

Skill Items

5. Write one way that tells how both objects are the same.

6. Write **2** ways that tell how object A is **different** from object B.

Object A   Object B

The faster the cab moves, the faster the wind blows on Herman.

7. Write the letter of the cab where the wind will blow fastest on Herman.

8. Write the letter of the cab where the wind will blow slowest on Herman.

A
25 miles per hour

B
10 miles per hour

C
30 miles per hour

D
45 miles per hour

E
35 miles per hour

Use the words in the box to write complete sentences.

| figure | thaw | distance | seven | moments |
| several | frozen | boiling | continued | circled |

9. ▮▮▮ paths ▮▮▮ for a great ▮▮▮.

10. ▮▮▮ water will ▮▮▮ ice in a few ▮▮▮.

Review Items

11. When a room gets colder, which way does the temperature go?

12. A car gets hotter. So what do you know about the temperature of the car?

The arrows show that the temperature is going down on thermometer **A** and going up on thermometer **B**.

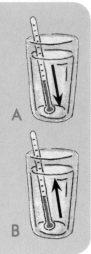

13. In which picture is the water getter colder, **A** or **B?**

14. In which picture is the water getter hotter, **A** or **B?**

15. Write the **name** of the city that's on the **west** coast.

16. Write the **name** of the city that's on the **east** coast.

17. Which letter shows where Chicago is?

18. Which letter shows where Denver is?

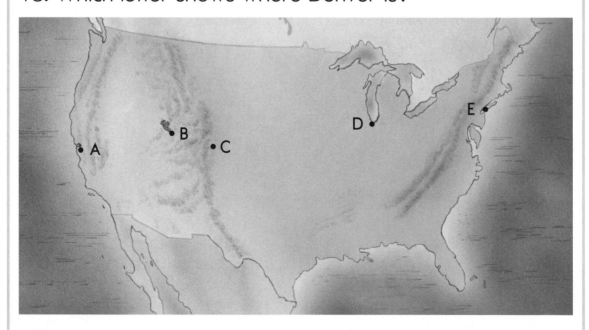

19. When we talk about how hot or cold something is, we tell about the ▮▮▮▮ of the thing.

   • weight   • temperature   • length

20. When the temperature goes up, the number of ▮▮▮▮ gets bigger.

   • miles   • degrees   • hours

21. What's the boiling temperature of water?

   • 212 miles   • 212 degrees   • 112 degrees

22. How fast does a jumbo jet fly?

   • 5 miles per hour   • 50 miles per hour
   • 500 miles per hour

23. The kitchen on an airplane is called ▮▮▮▮.

   • an alley   • a galley   • a kitchen

24. Does a housefly weigh **more than a gram** or **less than a gram?**

25. Does a table weigh **more than a gram** or **less than a gram?**

45

A

1
1. Pacific Ocean
2. Japan
3. enemy
4. attention
5. announcement

2
1. fastest
2. pushing
3. circled
4. warmer

3
1. headed
2. higher
3. ladies
4. wrapper

4
1. although
2. figure
3. copilot
4. taken

5
1. weren't
2. dodge
3. climb
4. huge
5. eager

6
1. blown
2. brave
3. June
4. gentlemen

B   # Airplanes and Wind

Look at the pictures on the next page.

All the planes in the picture can go 500 miles per hour if there is no wind. But there is a wind in each picture.

Here's the rule: The planes go the fastest when they go in the same direction the wind is blowing.

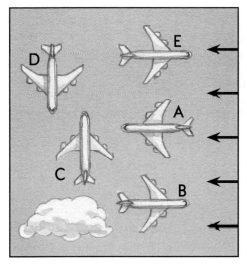

PICTURE 1

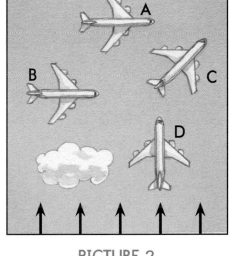

PICTURE 2

 Rough Air

Although Herman reached San Francisco in the middle of June, the air was cool because it was coming from a cool place. When Herman's jet landed, the temperature was only 63 degrees. An hour later, the temperature was 58 degrees, and the jet was ready to fly back to New York City.

A strong wind was blowing from the west. That wind was pushing big storm clouds over the United States. The captain of the jet plane knew about these clouds. He also knew that the jet would not be able to dodge them. The passengers were in for some rough air.

The captain said to his copilot, who sat next to him, "We're going to have some frightened passengers before this trip is over."

The captain was right. The jet took off and circled over the ocean. Then it turned and headed toward New York City. The jet began to climb higher and higher. Then it reached the huge clouds that had been blown in by the strong west wind. "Ladies and gentlemen," the captain said over the loudspeaker. "Please stay in your seat and keep your seat belt fastened. We are going to run into some rough. . ." The plane suddenly bounced. Then it dropped. "Oh," some of the people said. They began to hang onto their seats. The plane bounced ⭐ again and again.

It seemed as if the plane was going over a very, very rough road. Some of the passengers looked at the wings. The wings were bouncing up and down. A lot of the passengers were thinking the same thing. They thought, "We're going to crash," but they didn't say that. They tried to look brave. "This air is rough," they said with a smile. But they were not smiling inside.

The crew on the plane didn't mind the rough air very much. They knew that they would be out of the rough air as soon as they got above the clouds. They weren't the only ones who were not afraid. Herman had found a candy wrapper. And it was good, good, GOOD. The plane was much warmer now. And the food in the ovens was starting to thaw out. The smells of food filled the plane. While the passengers were thinking, "I'm going to be sick," Herman was thinking, "This place is good, good, GOOD."

The trip going to San Francisco had taken six hours. The trip back to New York took only five hours.

Can you figure out why?

MORE NEXT TIME

 Number your paper from 1 through 23.

Skill Items

Here are titles for different stories:
  a. The Man Who Stayed for Dinner
  b. Ten Ways to Trap Moles
  c. Mary Buys a Car

1. One story tells about a person who got something new. Write the letter of that title.

2. One story tells about a person who wanted to eat. Write the letter of that title.

3. One story tells about things you can do to catch some animals. Write the letter of that title.

Review Items

4. When a plane flies from New York City to San Francisco, is it flying in the **same direction** or the **opposite direction** as the wind?

5. Write the name of the city that's on the west coast.
6. Write the name of the city that's on the east coast.
7. Which letter shows where Chicago is?
8. Which letter shows where Salt Lake City is?

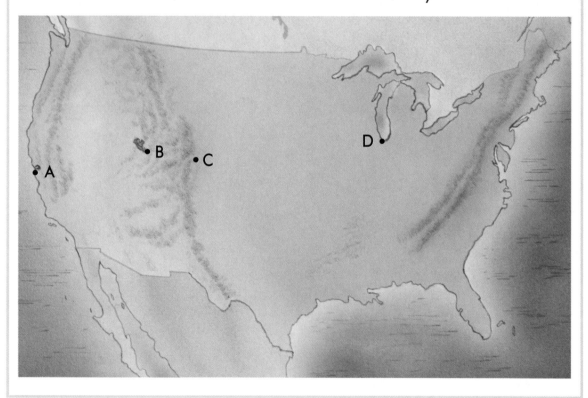

9. How many parts does the body of an insect have?

10. How many legs does an insect have?

11. How many legs does a spider have?

12. How many parts does a spider's body have?

Here's how fast different things can go:
- 20 miles per hour
- 35 miles per hour
- 200 miles per hour
- 500 miles per hour

13. Which speed tells how fast a fast man can run?

14. Which speed tells how fast a jet can fly?

15. Which speed tells how fast a fast dog can run?

16. Arrow B shows the direction the girl will jump. Which arrow shows the direction the boat will move?

R ⟶

S ⟵

17. What does the top of water have?

  • hair   • nails   • skin

18. If tiny animals fall from high places, they don't ▓▓▓▓.

19. The food that very small animals eat each day may weigh ▓▓▓▓.

  • 20 pounds   • 5 pounds   • more than the animal

20. If you get smaller, your voice gets ▓▓▓▓.

21. Jean got smaller. So what do you know about Jean's voice?

22. Does dew form in the middle of the day?

23. Dew forms when the air gets ▓▓▓▓.

  • cooler   • windy   • warmer

1
1. strength
2. human
3. mountain
4. excitement
5. California

2
1. sprayed
2. cleared
3. cooled
4. napped

3
1. several
2. continue
3. corners
4. hairy
5. enemy

4
1. Pacific Ocean
2. globe
3. jet's
4. free
5. web
6. strip

5
1. cross
2. Japan
3. attention
4. closets
5. mean-looking
6. moments

More About the World

In today's story you will read about a trip from New York City to San Francisco and then to Japan.

The map shows that trip.

Touch New York City and go to San Francisco.
In which direction did you go?
Now go from San Francisco to Japan.
In which direction did you go?
Is it farther from New York City to San Francisco or
from San Francisco to Japan?

Your teacher will show you a globe of the world. Find
New York City on that globe. Then go west from New
York City to San Francisco. Then go west from San
Francisco to Japan.

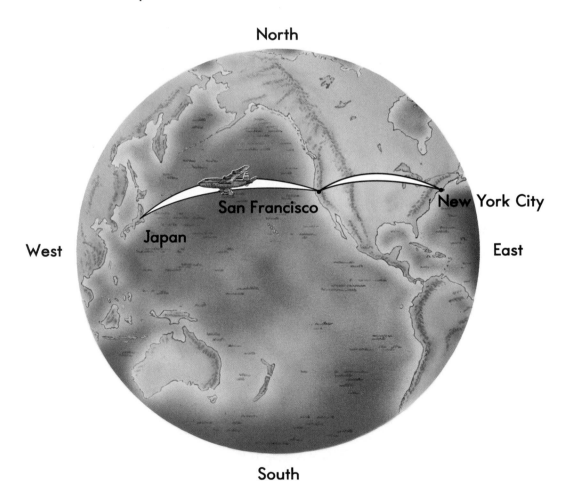

C Herman Heads to Japan

The jumbo jet landed at Kennedy Airport five hours after it took off from San Francisco. The passengers got off the plane, and the crew got off the plane. Workers came and sprayed the inside of the plane with insect spray. After the air cleared, there were six dead flies and one dead ant in the plane. But there was still one living fly. That fly had crawled inside one of the ovens. The oven had cooled some, but it was nice and warm.

Several hours later the oven was cool. Somebody opened it and Herman crawled out.

Passengers were coming into the plane. Some of the passengers were going to San Francisco. But some of them were going a lot farther. The jumbo jet was going to fly to San Francisco, and then it was going to continue to Japan.

After leaving San Francisco, the jet was going to cross a great ocean, called the Pacific Ocean. The trip from New York City to San Francisco is 25 hundred miles. After leaving San Francisco, a plane must fly west for another 5 thousand miles to get to Japan.

Look ⭐ at the map. It shows the world. Touch New York City on the map, and follow the jet's trip to San Francisco and then on to Japan.

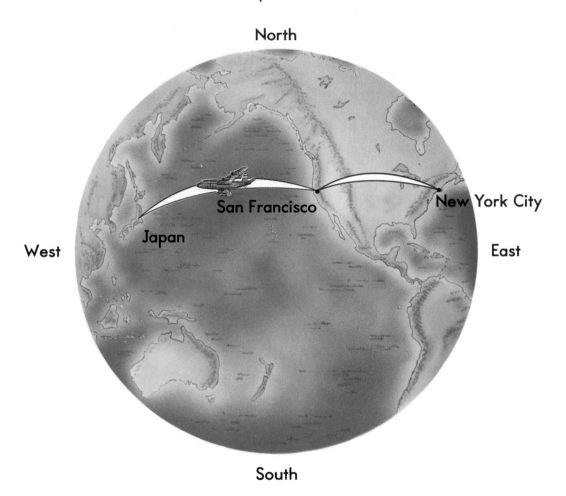

North

West

San Francisco

New York City

Japan

East

South

The trip to San Francisco took six hours. After the plane left San Francisco, the passengers napped and talked and ate. While they did that, Herman met an enemy. Herman was buzzing around near one of the coat closets in the jumbo jet. It was dark inside the coat closets, but some smells caught Herman's attention, so he buzzed inside one of the closets. He buzzed up into one of the corners. And then he kept trying to fly, but his legs were stuck to something. He buzzed his wings harder and harder. But he couldn't pull himself free. Once more, he buzzed. Time to rest.

Herman, like other flies, had big strange eyes that could see in all directions at the same time. Suddenly, Herman's eyes saw something moving toward him very fast. It was a large hairy thing with eight legs and a mean-looking mouth. Herman was stuck in a spider web, and the spider was ready to eat dinner.

MORE NEXT TIME

D **Number your paper from 1 through 23.**

Skill Items

> Here's a rule: **Fish live in water.**
> 1. A trout is a fish. So what does the rule tell you about a trout?
> 2. A frog is not a fish. So what does the rule tell you about a frog?

Review Items

3. What part of a car tells how fast the car is moving?

The speedometers are in 2 different cars.

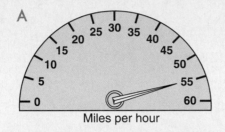
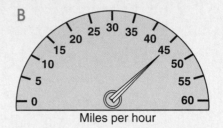

4. How fast is car A going?
5. How fast is car B going?
6. Which car is going faster?

7. Write the names of the 4 insects.
   - beetle   • bird   • spider   • fly   • ant
      • frog   • bee   • snake   • worm
8. When a glass of water gets colder, which way does the temperature go?
9. A pot gets hotter. So what do you know about the temperature of the pot?
10. When a plane flies from New York City to San Francisco, is it flying in the **same direction** or the **opposite direction** as the wind?

Write the letter of the plane in each picture that will go the fastest.

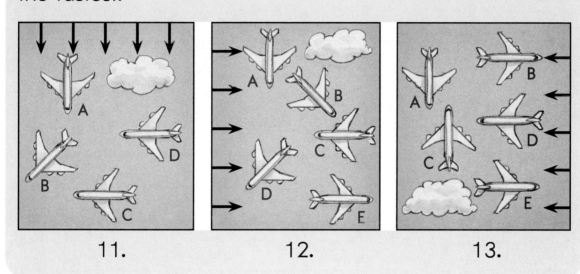

11.   12.   13.

14. Which arrow shows the way the cloud will move?

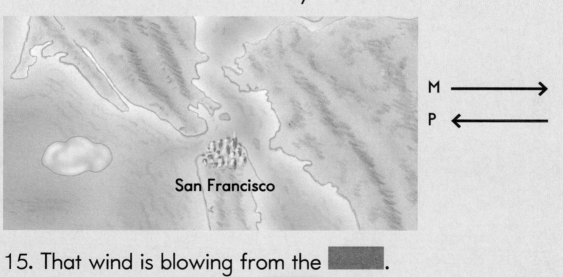

15. That wind is blowing from the ▮▮▮▮ .
16. So that wind is called a ▮▮▮▮ wind.

17. If a grain of sugar were very big, it would look like a box made of ███.

18. What kind of corners does a grain of sugar have?

19. You can see drops of water on grass early in the morning. What are those drops called?

20. Write the letter of each water strider.

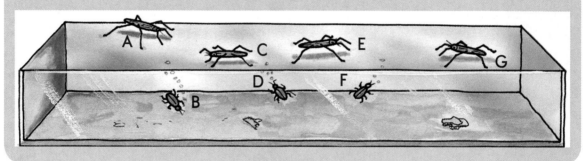

21. Write the letter of the ruler that will make the lowest sound.

22. Write the letter of the ruler that will make the highest sound.

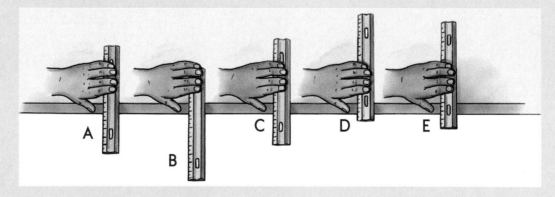

23. How fast does a jumbo jet fly?

- 50 miles per hour   • 500 miles per hour
- 5 miles per hour

1
1. Texas
2. Ohio
3. exit
4. sweat
5. poisonous
6. warm-blooded

2
1. tugged
2. biting
3. leaning
4. crowded
5. landing

3
1. moments
2. works
3. tries
4. strips
5. pens
6. papers

4
1. <u>distance</u>
2. <u>mummy</u>
3. <u>lucky</u>
4. <u>against</u>
5. <u>eager</u>

5
1. strength
2. slept
3. stuff
4. human
5. closet

6
1. announcement
2. California
3. excitement
4. freed
5. label

B The Eye of a Fly

If you look at a drop of water, you will see little pictures of things in the drop.

Look at the drop in the picture. You can see a window and a lamp in the drop.

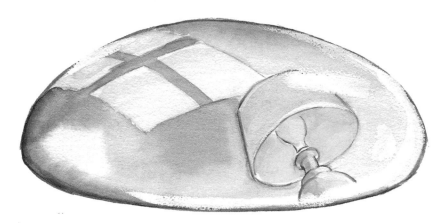

Your eye works like a drop. It is round and it catches pictures the same way the water drop catches pictures.

Look at the eye. You can see the picture the eye is catching.

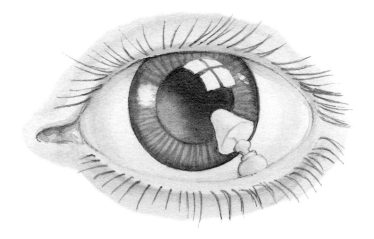

The eye of a fly is different from a human eye. Look at the fly in the picture. Below the fly is a large picture of the fly's eye.

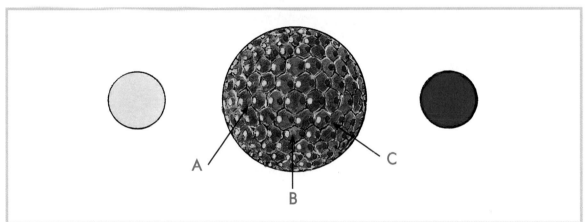

The eye of a fly is made up of many, many drops. Each drop catches a picture.

The fly's eye is catching pictures of a yellow dot and a blue dot.

Some drops on the eye catch a picture of the blue dot but not the yellow dot.

Some drops catch a picture of the yellow dot.

Some drops catch a picture of both dots.

Herman Tries to Escape

Herman was tired from trying to escape from the spider web, but when his eyes saw a big hairy spider moving toward him, Herman found a lot of strength. He buzzed harder than he had ever buzzed before. He tugged and pulled against the web. The web was sticky and it didn't let go of Herman's legs. But Herman kept trying.

Now the spider was trying to bite Herman and trying to wrap him up in a web. The spider was much bigger than Herman—three times bigger. The spider could walk on the web without getting stuck. But Herman was really stuck.

Most spiders kill insects by biting them. Then they wrap the insect in a web. The insect looks like a mummy. Later, the spider comes back and eats the best parts of the dead insect. The spider leaves the rest of the insect hanging in the web.

The passengers in the jumbo jet were talking to each other or leaning back in their seats thinking about what they would do when they reached Japan. Once in a while, passengers would look below at the ocean. They would think, "Ocean, ocean, ocean. All you can see is ocean."

While the passengers sat and talked and thought, Herman was fighting for his life.

Herman was lucky. The spider tried to turn Herman around and wrap him up. But when the spider turned Herman, the spider freed Herman's legs from the web. Herman gave a great buzz with his wings. Suddenly, he was in the air, with some sticky stuff still on his legs.

"Get out of that dark," Herman thought. He flew from the closet to the bright part of the jet. A moment later, Herman landed on a warm red and rubbed his front legs together. As Herman sat on the seat back, he did not remember what had just happened. For Herman, things were warm and red. And he was tired. Time to nap.

MORE NEXT TIME

D Number your paper from 1 through 25.

Story Items

1. Herman took a nap on something that was warm and red. What was it?

- an oven
- a closet
- a seat

2. In today's story the plane left San Francisco to go to ▮▮▮▮.

3. In which direction did the plane fly?

4. How far is it from San Francisco to that country?
   - 5 thousand miles
   - 5 hundred miles
   - 2 thousand miles

5. What ocean did the plane cross?

6. Why did Herman have a hard time escaping from the spider web?
   - His wings were stuck.
   - He couldn't see.
   - His legs were stuck.

7. How do most spiders kill insects?
   - by biting them
   - by crushing them
   - by wrapping them

8. Did the spider kill Herman?

Skill Items

Write the word or words from the box that mean the same thing as the underlined part of each sentence.

| continued | ahead | cook | figured out |
| pilot | decision | record | far apart | copilot |

9. The houses were <u>not close to each other</u>.
10. The <u>person in charge</u> of the plane told us where we were.
11. She <u>learned</u> how to put the table together.

They were eager to hear the announcement.

12. What word means **message?**
13. What word tells how they felt about hearing the announcement?

Review Items

14. How fast is truck **A** going?
15. How fast is truck **B** going?
16. Which truck is going faster?

A
50

B
30

17. How fast is boy C going?
18. How fast is boy D going?
19. Which boy is going faster?

5   8

20. Which arrow shows the way the air will leave the jet engines?
21. Which arrow shows the way the jet will move?

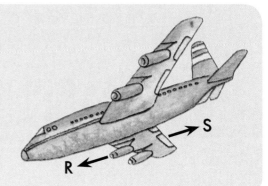

22. When the temperature goes up, the number of ▮ gets bigger.
   • miles   • degrees   • hours   • miles per hour

23. Write the letter of the animal that is facing into the wind.

24. Which direction is that animal facing?

25. So what's the **name** of that wind?

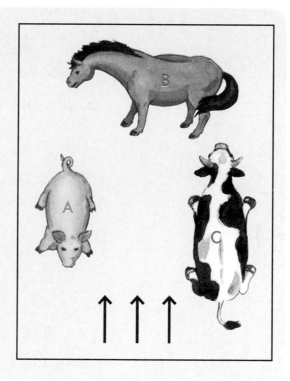

1
1. labeled
2. webs
3. marked
4. placed
5. disappeared

2
1. aisle
2. whole
3. eager
4. fist
5. Ohio

3
1. sweat
2. fifty
3. Texas
4. exit
5. country

4
1. poisonous
2. lifeboat
3. California
4. whirlpool

B ## Facts About Spiders

In the last Herman story, Herman met an enemy. What kind of animal was that enemy?

Here are facts you already know about spiders:

- Spiders are not insects.
- Spiders have eight legs, not six legs.

- The body of a spider has two parts, not three.

Here are some new facts about spiders:
- Many spiders make webs to catch insects.
- Some spiders are bigger than your fist.
- Most spiders are not poisonous to people.

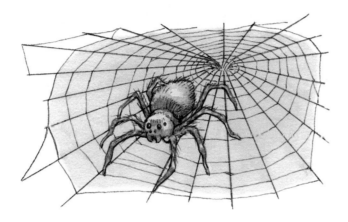

C The Size of Some States

The United States is a **country.** It is called the United States because it is made up of many **states.** There are fifty states in the United States. The map shows the states that are in the United States. Four states are labeled.

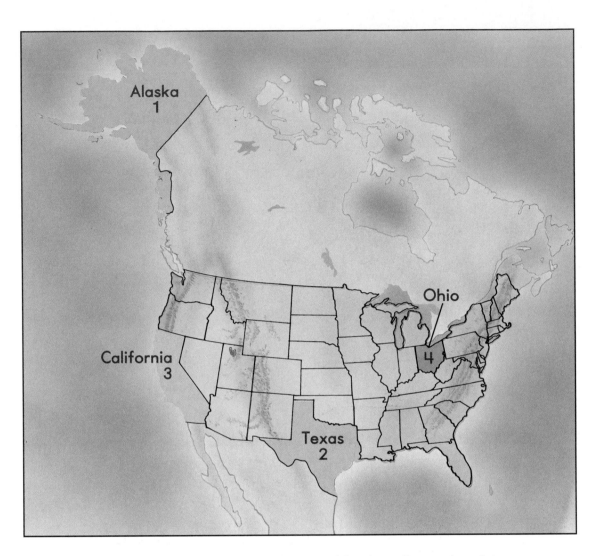

The state that is marked **1** is Alaska. It is the biggest state in the United States.

State **2** is Texas. It is the second biggest state.

State **3** is the third biggest state. What is the name of that state?

State **4** is one of the smaller states. Its name is Ohio.

Do you know the name of the state that you live in?
The United States is much bigger than the country of Japan. The whole country of Japan is smaller than the state of Alaska. The picture shows what the whole country of Japan would look like if it were placed next to Alaska.

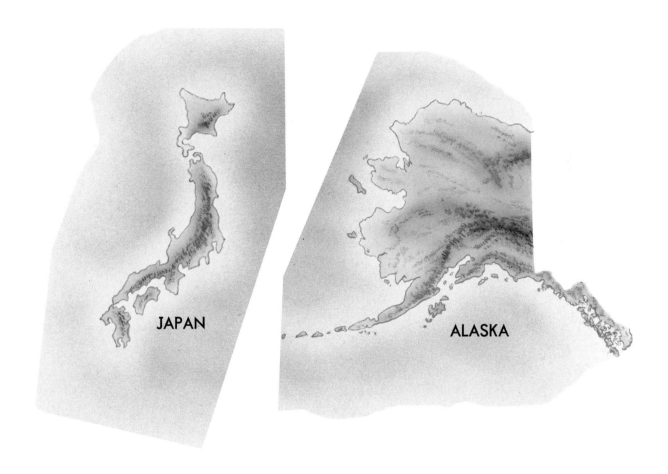

JAPAN

ALASKA

The Jumbo Jet Lands in Japan

Herman had just escaped from a spider web and he was on a warm red seat back. For Herman it was a time to nap. But for the passengers, it was a time for excitement. Off in the distance were green strips of land and a great mountain with a white top. "It's Japan," the passengers said to themselves.

The plane was no longer six miles above the earth. It was less than a mile above the earth and it continued to get lower as it approached the land. "Look at those tiny lines down there," one of the passengers said and pointed. "That's the airport."

Now the passengers began to get ready for the plane's landing. Some people fixed their hair. Others put away their pens and papers. Every few moments, they looked out the ★ windows again. "It's beautiful," they said. It was. As the passengers felt this excitement, Herman slept.

Japan is a small country compared to the United States. But many people live in Japan. Japan is smaller than the state of Alaska. But there are more people in Japan than there are in these three states put together: Texas, Alaska, and Ohio.

The passengers on the plane were eager to leave. After the plane was on the ground, the passengers lined up and slowly moved toward the exit door.

Herman slept through this excitement. He slept until the plane became cool.

MORE NEXT TIME

E Number your paper from 1 through 23.

Skill Items

Use the words in the box to write complete sentences.

strength	eager	enemy	boiling	announcement
	thaw	free	moments	cross

1. ▨ water will ▨ ice in a few ▨.
2. They were ▨ to hear the ▨.

3. Look at object A and object B. Write one way that tells how both objects are the same.

4. Write **2** ways that tell how object A is **different** from object B.

Object A

Object B

Review Items

5. A mile is around ▨ feet.
   - 5 hundred   • 5 thousand   • 1 thousand

6. A speedometer tells about ▨.
   - hours   • miles per hour   • miles

7. How many legs does an insect have?

8. How many legs does a fly have?

9. How many legs does a bee have?

10. How many legs does a spider have?

11. How many parts does a spider's body have?

12. How many parts does a fly's body have?

13. Some of the objects in the picture are insects, and some are spiders. Write the letter of each spider.

14. Write the letter of each insect.

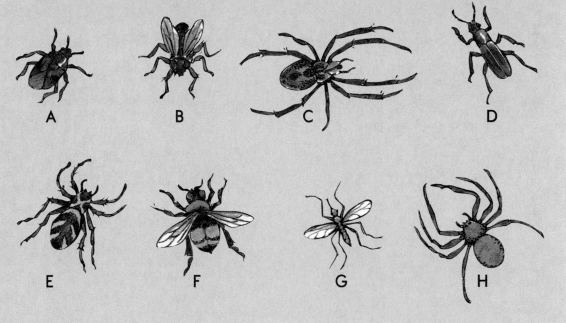

15. Object D is not a spider. Tell why.

Here's how fast different things can go:
- 20 miles per hour
- 35 miles per hour
- 200 miles per hour
- 500 miles per hour

16. Which speed tells how fast a fast man can run?

17. Which speed tells how fast a fast dog can run?

18. Which speed tells how fast a jet can fly?

19. Which eye works like one drop, a human's eye or a fly's eye?

20. Which eye works like many drops, a human's eye or a fly's eye?

21. Which eye can see more things at the same time, a human's eye or a fly's eye?

Things that are this far apart ←→ on the map are 2 miles apart.

Things that are this far apart ←——→ on the map are 4 miles apart.

22. How far is it from the pool to the store?

23. How far is it from the park to the bus stop?

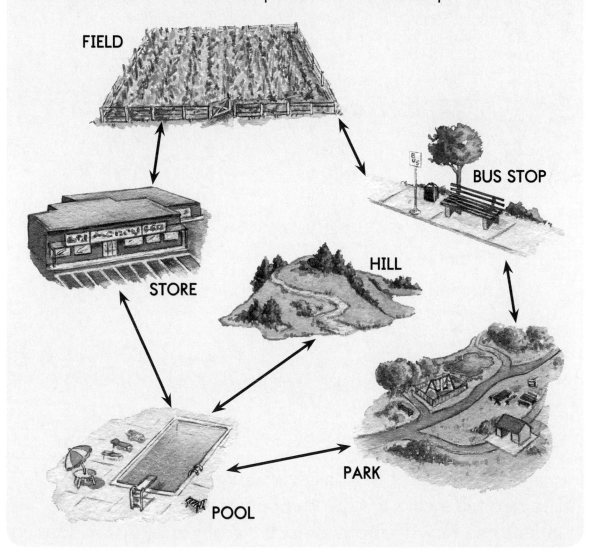

A

1
1. Italy
2. Turkey
3. China
4. million
5. earth

2
1. butterflies
2. changes
3. fleas
4. rabbits
5. robins

3
1. eager
2. warm-blooded
3. cold-blooded
4. exit
5. lined

4
1. slowing
2. sweat
3. unless
4. visiting
5. aisle

B   Herman Is Cold-Blooded

Herman hated cold things. You can understand why flies don't like cold things or cool weather if you understand how flies are different from humans or dogs.

All insects are cold-blooded. Flies are insects. So flies are cold-blooded. Here are some other animals that are cold-blooded: ants, fleas, spiders, frogs, and butterflies.

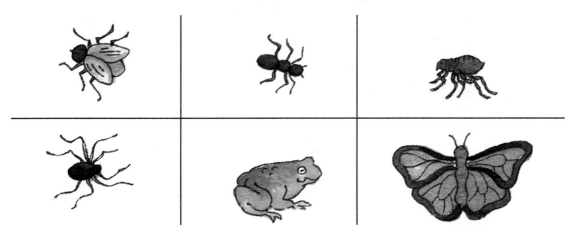

Cold-blooded animals are different from warm-blooded animals. Here are some animals that are warm-blooded: robins, dogs, rabbits, cows, humans, horses, and deer.

If an animal is warm-blooded, the temperature inside that animal's body always stays the same. If the outside temperature goes up, the inside temperature does not change. If the outside temperature goes down, the inside temperature does not change.

If an animal is cold-blooded, the inside temperature of that animal changes when the outside temperature changes. If the outside temperature goes up, what happens to the inside temperature?

If the outside temperature goes down, what happens to the inside temperature?

Humans are warm-blooded. Your body temperature is always around 98 degrees. When the air outside is 15 degrees below zero, your fingers may get cold. Your feet may feel very cold. But the inside of your body is 98 degrees. When the temperature outside is 90 degrees, you may feel ✸ very warm and sticky. You may sweat. But the inside of your body is still 98 degrees.

Flies are different. Their inside temperature changes as the temperature outside their body changes. When the air is 90 degrees outside, the inside of the fly is 90 degrees. When the air is 45 degrees outside, you know the temperature inside the fly.

❀ Because flies work this way, they have a problem: Their body slows down when it gets cold. Try catching a fly on a warm day. It is hard to do because the fly is fast. The fly is fast because everything inside the fly's body is hot and is working fast.

Try catching a fly when the weather is very cool. The fly is slow and easy to catch. The fly is slow because everything inside the fly's body is cool and is working very slowly. Remember: A fly's body slows down when it gets cold.

Herman didn't know this ✿ rule. He did know that he didn't like cool places and he didn't like dark places unless they were warm. He was in Japan. He wanted to leave the jet because it was getting too cool for him. The air temperature was down to 45 degrees. He was slowing down. And his eyes could see that something was coming toward him.

MORE TO COME

C Number your paper from 1 through 18.

Skill Items

Here's a rule: **The colder the temperature, the slower the insects move.**

1. Write the letter of the insect that will move the slowest.
2. Write the letter of the insect that will move the fastest.

A

60 degrees

B

45 degrees

C

30 degrees

D

95 degrees

E

50 degrees

Review Items

3. When we talk about miles per hour, we tell how ▮▮▮ something is moving.

4. Which object is the hottest?
5. What is the temperature of that object?

A
45 degrees

B
30 degrees

C
60 degrees

6. When the temperature goes up, the number of ▮▮▮ gets bigger.
   - miles per hour   - hours   - miles   - degrees
7. How many legs does an insect have?
8. How many legs does an ant have?
9. How many legs does a spider have?
10. How many parts does a spider's body have?
11. How many parts does a fly's body have?

12. Which letter shows where San Francisco is?
13. Which letter shows where New York City is?
14. Which letter shows where the Pacific Ocean is?
15. Which letter shows where Japan is?
16. Is the United States shown on this map?

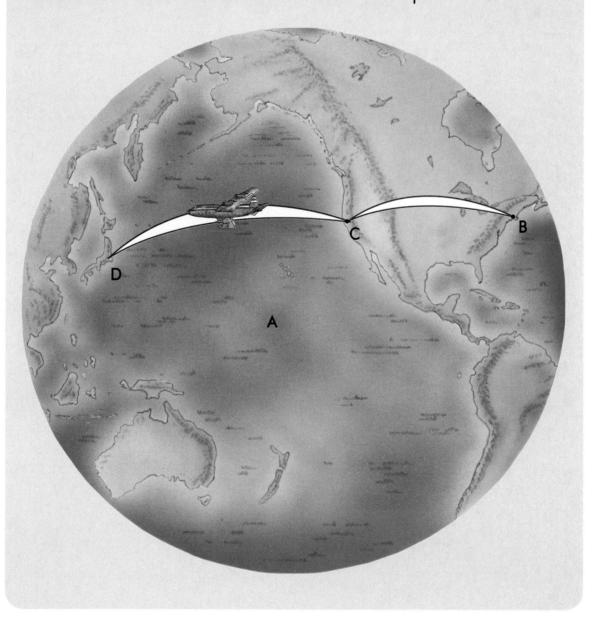

Some of the objects in the picture are insects, and some are spiders.

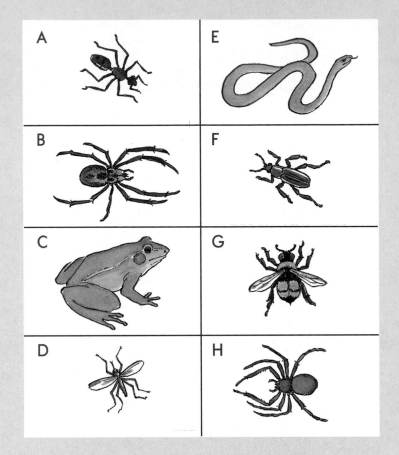

17. Write the letters of the spiders.
18. Write the letters of the insects.

Number your paper from 1 through 33.

Here's how fast different things can go:
- 20 miles per hour
- 200 miles per hour
- 35 miles per hour
- 500 miles per hour

1. Which speed tells how fast a fast man can run?

2. Which speed tells how fast a jet can fly?

3. Which speed tells how fast a fast dog can run?

4. When an object gets hotter, the temperature goes ▮▮▮.

The arrows show that the temperature is going up on thermometer A and going down on thermometer B.

5. In which picture is the water getting colder, **A** or **B?**

6. In which picture is the water getting hotter, **A** or **B?**

A

B

7. Which letter shows where San Francisco is?

8. If you were in San Francisco, which direction would you face if you wanted the wind to blow in your face?

9. When a plane flies from New York City to San Francisco, is it flying in the **same direction** or the **opposite direction** as the wind?

10. Which letter shows where New York City is?
11. Which letter shows where San Francisco is?
12. Which letter shows where Japan is?
13. Which letter shows where the Pacific Ocean is?

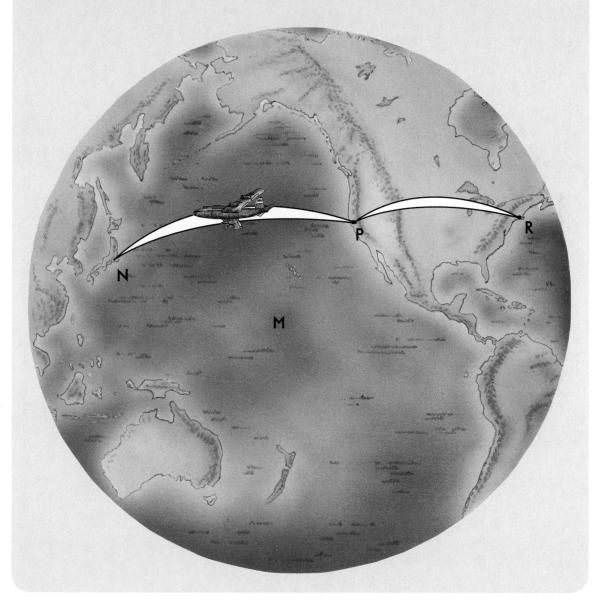

Write **W** for warm-blooded animals and **C** for cold-blooded animals.

14. beetle

15. camel

16. spider

17. dog

18. fly

19. What's the boiling temperature of water?

  • 212 miles • 112 degrees • 212 degrees

20. Write the letter of the animal that is facing into the wind.

21. Which direction is that animal facing?

22. So what's the **name** of that wind?

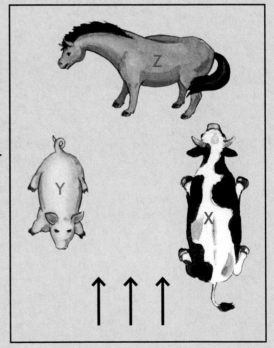

23. How many states are in the United States?

24. The biggest state in the United States is .

25. The second-biggest state in the United States is ▮▮▮.
26. How far is it from San Francisco to Japan?

Skill Items

For each item, write the underlined word or words from the sentences in the box.

> <u>Several</u> paths <u>continued</u> for a great <u>distance</u>.
> <u>Boiling</u> water will <u>thaw</u> ice in a few <u>moments</u>.
> They were <u>eager</u> to hear the <u>announcement</u>.

27. What underlining means **melt?**
28. What underlining means **message?**
29. What underlining means **kept on going?**
30. What underlining refers to more than two but less than a lot?
31. What underlining tells how they felt about hearing the announcement?

Here's a rule: **Every spider has eight legs.**
32. Keb is a spider. So what does the rule tell you about Keb?
33. Bop is not a spider. So what does the rule tell you about Bop?

END OF TEST 5

Fact Game Answer Key

Lesson 30

2. a. no
   b. cooler
3. 10 cows
4. 5 thousand
5. a. D (or G)
   b. 1 mile
   c. 1 mile
6. United States
7. a. 25 hundred miles
   b. 13 hundred miles
8. a. week
   b. minute
   c. year
9. a. inches
   b. miles
   c. meters
10. a. Q
    b. M
11. dew
12. glass

Lesson 40

2. J, K, M
3. L, P
4. grams
5. a. 40 miles per hour
   b. 60 miles per hour
   c. B
6. 25 hundred miles
7. a. how far
   b. how fast
8. a. C
   b. A
9. fast
10. in the opposite direction
11. A, D, F
12. smaller; higher

Lesson 50

2. a. cow
   b. north
   c. north wind

3. a. 35 miles per hour
   b. 500 miles per hour
   c. 20 miles per hour

4. a. 80 degrees
   b. 40 degrees

5. ant, flea, bee, beetle

6. a. New York City
   b. Japan

7. c. Pacific Ocean
   d. San Francisco

8. a. 25 hundred miles
   b. 5 thousand miles

9. a. 50
   b. Alaska

10. a. T
    b. R

11. 212 degrees

12. from the west to the east

VOCABULARY SENTENCES

1. You measure your weight in pounds.

2. They waded into the stream to remove tadpoles.

3. The fly boasted about escaping from the spider.

4. The workers propped up the cage with steel bars.

5. Hunters were stationed at opposite ends of the field.

6. He motioned to the flight attendant ahead of him.

7. The traffic was moving forty miles per hour.

8. He is supposed to make a decision in a couple of days.

9. Several paths continued for a great distance.

10. Boiling water will thaw ice in a few moments.

11. They were eager to hear the announcement.

12. The lifeboat disappeared in the whirlpool.